The Shaper Book

D1082342

The Shaper Book

LONNIE BIRD

The Taunton Press

Front and back cover photos: Lonnie Bird

Taunton
BOOKS & VIDEOS
for fellow enthusiasts

© 1996 by The Taunton Press, Inc.
All rights reserved.

First printing: 1996
Printed in the United States of America

A FINE WOODWORKING Book

FINE WOODWORKING® is a trademark of the Taunton Press, Inc.,
registered in the U.S. Patent and Trademark Office.

The Taunton Press, 63 South Main Street, Box 5506,
Newtown, CT 06470-5506

Library of Congress Cataloging-in-Publication Data

Bird, Lonnie.
   The shaper book / Lonnie Bird.
   p.   cm.
   "A Fine woodworking book" —
   Includes index.
   ISBN 1-56158-120-8
   1. Shapers.   2. Woodwork.   I. Title.
TT186.B517 1996
684'.08—dc20   96-35740
                                                    CIP

To my loving wife, Linda

Acknowledgments

I would like to thank the following people at The Taunton Press for their help in producing this book: Helen Albert, who believed in this project and made it possible; acquisitions editor Rick Peters, who gave me constructive criticism and helpful feedback; and editor Tom McKenna, whose efforts made this book organized and understandable.

For help with photography, I'd like to thank two of my former students: David Robinson and Eric Jacobsen.

Many people gave me technical assistance, including Rick Paul of Charles G.G. Schmidt, Jim Brewer of Freud, Tom Freeborn of Freeborn, Inc., Renata Mastrofrancesco of Delta Machinery, and Cliff Paddock of CMT Tools.

Most of all, I would like to thank my wife, Linda. Her expertise with the computer coupled with her limitless support made her a true partner in putting together this book.

Contents

Introduction

The shaper is one of the most productive, yet least understood of all woodworking machines. Many woodworkers I've talked to think that the shaper is dangerous or that they can perform the same functions with their table-mounted router. While these statements have some merit, they are not entirely true.

The purpose of this book is to show the vast possibilities of this overlooked machine. More than just a treatise on shaper techniques, this book also gives practical examples of how the shaper can be put to use.

It's my sincere desire that the techniques in this book will help you discover for yourself the full potential of the shaper and expand your woodworking skills.

A word about safety

I've spent many hours working to provide safe information in this book. However, as it says in the beginning of *Fine Woodworking* magazine, "Working wood is inherently dangerous. Don't try to perform operations you learned about here (or elsewhere) until you are certain that they are safe for you and your shop situation."

I follow the guideline, "If it doesn't feel safe, don't do it." Many of the techniques in this book are advanced and should only be attempted in lieu of this advice.

1

Introduction to the Shaper

If you've ever used a table-mounted router to shape small moldings or to make raised panels, in essence you've used a small shaper. Many of the operating principles and even the cutterhead profiles are similar. But the largest router is no match for the shaper in terms of raw power. A large cutterhead for the router is really just a small cutterhead for the shaper, and while the router will whine and bog down in a heavy cut, the shaper will breeze right through. Because the shaper has a much larger motor and outweighs the router by several hundred pounds, it can cut much heavier molding profiles and at the same time create a smoother finished surface than the router.

With the right jigs, fixtures and tooling, the shaper can become a highly flexible machine, capable of broadening the scope of your woodworking. Over the years I've learned to rely heavily on my shaper for everything from small moldings to large panels for architectural doors. By making several cuts on the same piece of stock, I can make very large, complex moldings like those typically produced on an industrial molder. I also use my shaper for making curved moldings for furniture and circular-head doorways. Mounted with a stub spindle and cope cutterhead, the shaper does an excellent job of coping the ends of rails for cope-and-stick sash and doors.

This 3-hp shaper with a ¾-in. spindle accepts a wide array of cutters, fences and jigs to handle many different applications—from small moldings to large panels for architectural doors.

The shaper can also increase production in custom woodworking situations by eliminating tedious handwork. A pencil-post bed is a good example. Years ago, the posts were shaped by hand with spokeshaves and planes, and the job of shaping four posts for a bed could take hours. However, I can shape four posts in less than 10 minutes with the shaper and a jig to position the posts. Making furniture with curved parts often involves tiresome removal of bandsawed edges with files and sandpaper. Equipped with a ball-bearing rub collar and a template, the shaper will smooth or mold the edges in a fraction of the time.

Despite all the shaper's positive qualities, it has always had a reputation for being dangerous. Like any large power woodworking tool, the shaper has inherent dangers. But the shaper can also be a safe and extremely productive machine when properly set up and used.

THE SHAPER

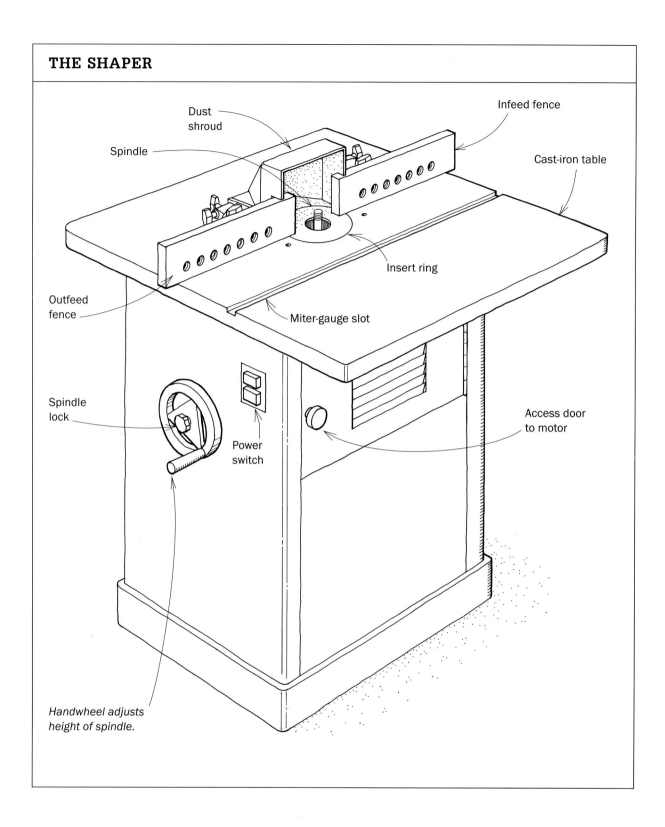

Dust shroud

Spindle

Infeed fence

Cast-iron table

Insert ring

Outfeed fence

Miter-gauge slot

Spindle lock

Power switch

Access door to motor

Handwheel adjusts height of spindle.

Shaper Anatomy

At first glance the shaper seems simple—a spindle protruding through a hole in the center of the table. But the cutterheads, fences and jigs provide a wide variety of applications. If you haven't yet purchased a shaper, this section will give you an idea of what to look for in a machine. The main parts of the shaper that will affect the price and performance are the spindle, the motor, the fence and the table.

SPINDLE

The spindle is the heart of the shaper; it drives the cutterhead, and its size determines the machine's capabilities and limitations. The shaper's spindle size is one reason why the machine outperforms the router. The largest routers will accept only a ½-in. diameter shank bit. In contrast, shaper spindles—sized in ¼-in. increments—range from ½ in. to 1½ in. in diameter. The large spindle size not

Changing Spindles

One of the features I look for in a shaper is interchangeable spindles. It's a tremendous asset, especially if you want to run a cope cutterhead on a stub spindle occasionally to make sash and doors. On most shapers, changing spindles is easy.

Open the access door to the motor, and you'll see a tapered nut at the spindle base. Remove the nut and slide the spindle out of the arbor. If the spindle seems stuck, gently tap it with a rubber mallet at the spindle base to free it up. Now remove the threaded rod from the spindle base and thread it into the next spindle.

When inserting the new spindle, notice that it contains a keyway that must align with a small pin in the arbor. The keyway prevents the spindle from spinning within the arbor. Install the tapered nut, with the taper positioned up toward the spindle, and tighten it firmly. If several months pass between spindle changes, it's a good idea to wipe a light film of oil over the spindle base before installing it in the arbor. I learned this the hard way when I had difficulty removing a stubborn spindle. When I finally removed it, I discovered a light coating of rust, which had locked the spindle firmly in the arbor.

When changing spindles, align the keyway in the spindle with the pin in the arbor.

The handwheel on the side of the shaper makes adjusting the spindle height easy.

Most ¾-in. shapers have interchangeable spindles. A ¾-in. spindle (chucked in shaper) is good for heavy cuts. The ½-in. stub spindle (middle) is ideal for coping. And the ½-in. spindle (right) is adequate for light-duty work.

only dampens vibration and allows the shaper to cut wide moldings, but the long length of the spindle also reaches to the center of wide stock on edge. For even greater reach, you can order an extra-long spindle.

A handwheel on the side of the machine makes precise height adjustments to the spindle quick and easy. Handwheel movement should be smooth and precise to make fine adjustments to the cutting depth. A lock, usually located in the center of the handwheel, prevents the spindle height from creeping out of adjustment while you are shaping.

As you might expect, the midsized machines are best suited for custom woodworking, both in price and capability. The ½-in. machines are underpowered and prone to excessive vibration and spindle deflection, where the spindle flexes slightly during a heavy cut. The 1¼-in. and 1½-in. spindle machines have enormous power (and a high price tag), and if you are planning to do production

An optional extra-long spindle provides greater reach on wider, thick stock.

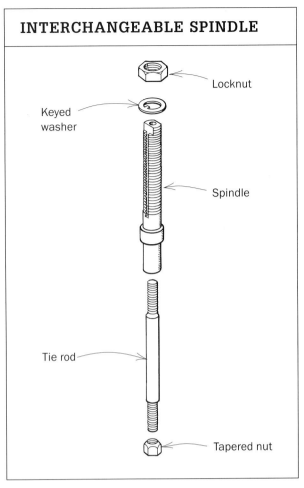

INTERCHANGEABLE SPINDLE

Locknut

Keyed washer

Spindle

Tie rod

Tapered nut

work or very large moldings for architectural woodwork, you'll need all the power you can get; otherwise, the extra power will most likely be overkill. Besides, the cutterheads required for large machines will take a huge bite out of your woodworking budget.

I've found that a ¾-in. spindle shaper is an ideal size for the average woodworking shop. Most ¾-in. shapers have interchangeable spindles that greatly increase their versatility (see the drawing above). A ¾-in. spindle is large enough to withstand the loads of heavy panel-raising and similar cuts without excessive vibration. My ¾-in. machine also has several interchangeable spindles, including a ½-in. stub spindle for coping.

If you plan to do cope-and-stick joinery, a stub spindle is a good investment. The reason for this is a standard spindle is threaded externally. When the cutterhead is secured with a nut, the spindle will extend up past the cutterhead and interfere with a cut such as coping the shoulder of a long tenon. However, the stub spindle

is threaded internally, and the cutterhead is secured with a cap screw. Furthermore, because the cope cutterhead is counterbored, the cap screw is flush with the top. This neat design will allow you to cope traditional mortise-and-tenon joinery regardless of the tenon length, which is extremely useful for frame-and-panel and sash construction.

One of the most important features of a shaper is a reversing switch for changing spindle rotation (see the photo above). Changing the spindle rotation prevents tearout. Shaper spindles typically turn in a counterclockwise direction, and the stock is fed from right to left, against the spindle rotation. (For safety reasons, don't ever feed the stock in the same direction as the spindle rotation without a power feeder. A power feeder is an optional accessory that uses motor-driven wheels to push stock through the shaper.) When shaping, it's important to cut in the direction of the grain, just as when hand-planing or jointing the edge of a board. For safety reasons, most cutterheads are mounted to run from underneath the stock so that the stock will cover the cutterhead and shield your hands. But there are some cutterheads designed to cut

Power is transferred to the spindle (left in photo) from the motor through a belt and pulleys.

on top of the stock. With a reversing spindle, you can invert the cutterhead and reverse the spindle rotation, making this cutterhead safer. This isn't always possible with a machine that turns counterclockwise only.

Reversing the spindle rotation will also allow you to cut with the grain on curved stock. Because curved stock changes grain direction, it often must be shaped from two directions to cut "downhill" and achieve the smoothest cut. A reversing switch will allow you to do this easily.

MOTOR

A shaper's motor sits off to the side below the cutterhead, and power is transferred to the spindle from the motor by a belt and pulleys (see the photo above). A good-quality shaper will be able to run at multiple speeds to accommodate cutterheads of various diameters. At minimum, the shaper should have at least two speeds, with a low speed no higher than 7,000 revolutions per minute (rpm). A large industrial machine usually has several speeds, with a low of around 3,000 rpm.

A small-diameter cutterhead has a slower rim speed than a large-diameter cutterhead when run at the same rpm, and so a higher rpm is needed to increase the rim speed to produce a smooth surface. (This is one reason why a router runs at such high rpm.) On the other hand, because a large cutterhead removes so much stock in a single pass, it must be run at a lower rpm to reduce the rim speed. This way the surface doesn't get burned. Running a large cutterhead too fast is unsafe (these cutterheads have a specified maximum rpm) and may burn or burnish the stock. (Burnishing causes the wood surface to become glazed. It can occur when the feed rate is too slow for the rpm of the cutterhead.)

Also, don't overlook the importance of the power switch. It should be large and mounted in an easy-to-reach location. I also prefer a low-voltage, magnetic switch for safety. During the occasional power failure, a magnetic switch will break contact, preventing accidental startup when power is restored.

FENCE

The shaper fence plays a two-part role: It safely guides the stock past the cutterhead and limits the depth of cut. Shaper manufacturers provide a split fence, which allows the infeed and outfeed halves to be adjusted independently (see the left photo below). When shaping the entire edge of a workpiece, the outfeed fence must be forward of the infeed fence to support the stock.

A split fence allows the infeed and outfeed halves to be adjusted independently. The fence is secured with bolts that fit into threaded holes in the shaper table.

The dust shroud surrounds the cutterhead and directs the shavings toward the dust collector.

This simple shop-made fence is made of two pieces of plywood and covered with laminate to reduce friction. Clamps hold the assembly to the table.

This prevents the trailing end of the stock from being sniped (reduced in width at the end). The fence is secured with bolts that fit into threaded holes in the shaper table. The size of the opening between the fence halves is also adjustable. For safety and accuracy, the opening should be as small as possible. A dust shroud between the fence halves surrounds the cutterhead and directs the shavings toward the dust collector (see the right photo on the facing page).

Although I find the split fence provided with the shaper useful, I also find it to be limiting at times. A variety of shop-made custom fences greatly increases the safety and versatility of the shaper. A simple straight fence eliminates having to realign the finicky split-fence halves (see the photo above). I have two such fences, each with a different-size opening for various cutterhead diameters. I secure the fence to the shaper table with a pair of clamps. When shaping long molding strips, an extended fence that reaches beyond the shaper table will prevent the stock from sagging and ruining the cut (see the drawing on p. 16).

To use large-diameter cutterheads with the split fence, you must open the fence wide enough to expose the cutterhead to the stock, which also exposes it to your hands. I don't know about you, but passing my hands a few inches from a large, spinning mass of steel and sharp edges makes me nervous. That's why I use the shop-made box fence shown on p. 17. It provides a solid barrier between my

EXTENDED FENCE

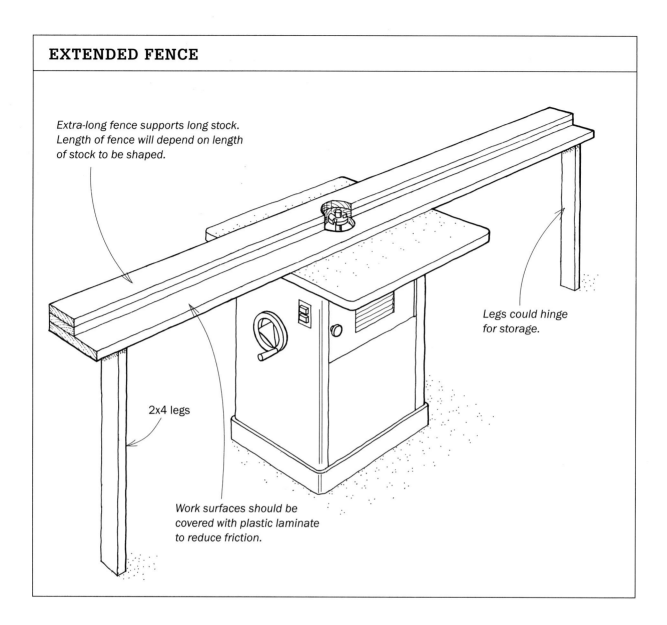

Extra-long fence supports long stock. Length of fence will depend on length of stock to be shaped.

Legs could hinge for storage.

2x4 legs

Work surfaces should be covered with plastic laminate to reduce friction.

hands and the cutterhead while allowing the stock to slip under the front of the box. The base of the box works as a guide and is made of ¼-in. plywood. The opening around the spindle is very small—just a fraction larger than the spindle size—which prevents the stock from dropping into the fence opening. Because the stock slides under the box front, the cutterhead is totally enclosed.

When shaping small parts, it is best to shape oversize stock, then reduce it in size. However, sometimes this isn't possible. To prevent small stock from catching onto the outfeed half of a split fence and dropping into the fence opening, I use a zero-clearance fence (see the photo on p. 18). To make this fence, I fasten a ¼-in. plywood

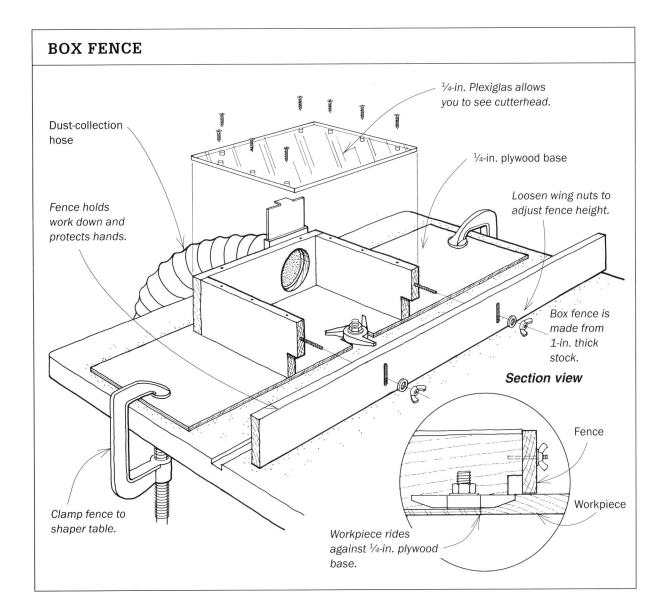

¼-in. Plexiglas allows you to see cutterhead.

Dust-collection hose

¼-in. plywood base

Loosen wing nuts to adjust fence height.

Fence holds work down and protects hands.

Box fence is made from 1-in. thick stock.

Section view

Fence

Clamp fence to shaper table.

Workpiece rides against ¼-in. plywood base.

Workpiece

strip to the split fence and create an opening. To do this, secure one end of the fence, turn on the shaper, then slowly and carefully pivot the fence into the cutterhead. Stop when enough cutterhead is exposed to produce the cut, shut off the power and secure the other end of the fence. The resulting fence will give a great deal more support than the standard split fence. Of course, you'll still need a jig so that you can hold and feed the small stock safely (for more on jigs for the shaper, see Chapter 11).

Shop-made fences are easily constructed with plywood and medium-density fiberboard (MDF). I use quick and simple butt

A zero-clearance fence prevents small stock from catching on the outfeed half of a split fence and falling into the spindle opening.

joinery reinforced with screws and glue. To reduce wear and friction, I cover the work surfaces with plastic laminate.

TABLE

The table on a shaper should be made of cast iron to add mass and to keep vibration to a minimum. I once purchased a shaper with a heavy-gauge sheet-metal top. It was a reasonably priced European import. Since my budget was limited, I figured it was worth a try. The distributor had a 30-day refund policy, so the experiment was risk-free, at least from a monetary standpoint (if not from a safety standpoint).

When the shaper arrived, I unpacked it in anticipation. The machine had a ¾-in. spindle and the power to push it. The parts seemed well-machined. But without the weight and mass of a cast-iron table, it vibrated excessively. What a disappointment! At the very least, the vibration affected the quality of the cut. But when mounted with large cutterheads, the shaper roared loudly with vibration. Needless to say, I took advantage of the return policy.

A shaper table should be sized according to the spindle diameter. Large-diameter spindles require a large table not only to support the work but also to add mass and to reduce vibration generated by large cutterheads. Some machines have holes, which allow you to mount extension wings to increase the table size. This option is especially important if you plan to shape curved stock, which requires support on all sides of the spindle rather than just in front, as is the case with straight stock. Beware of shapers with large (¾ in. to 1 in.) spindles and small tables. Shaping stock without adequate table support can be frustrating as well as dangerous.

INSERT RINGS

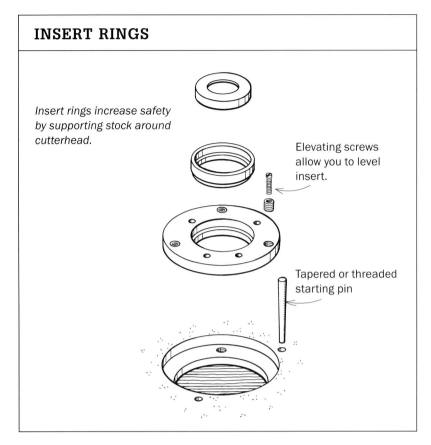

Insert rings increase safety by supporting stock around cutterhead.

Elevating screws allow you to level insert.

Tapered or threaded starting pin

The starting pin supports curved stock when shaping without a fence.

Most shapers have two or three insert rings around the spindle for increasing and decreasing the size of the opening in the table (see the drawing above). Large cutterheads will require that you remove one or two rings to allow the cutterhead to clear the opening during operation. However, the rings should be replaced when using smaller cutterheads to give adequate support to the stock. The insert rings should fit snugly within the opening and should sit flush with the shaper top.

Most shapers have a miter-gauge slot and several threaded holes machined in the table to accept a starting pin. The miter-gauge slot (³⁄₈ in. by ¾ in. is the standard size) is most useful as a guide for jigs, especially when shaping end grain. The starting pin is simply a smooth, steel rod that fits into a tapered hole in the table (see the photo above) and is used to support curved stock when shaping without a fence. It is an extremely important accessory for shaping curved stock, but if your machine did not come with one, you can order a pin or use a threaded bolt for the same purpose.

Check if the spindle is square to the table by mounting a straightedge between two collars. Then lower the spindle until the straightedge just touches the table.

Check if the insert rings are flush with the table surface by placing the edge of a straightedge across the rings and the table.

Tuning the Shaper

Like other woodworking machines, the shaper performs better when properly tuned. Fortunately, tuning the shaper is simple, especially when compared to complex machines, such as the table saw or planer. Basically, there are three things to check for when tuning the shaper.

By far the most critical adjustment is squaring the spindle to the table. This relationship is especially important when shaping with matching cutterheads, such as cope-and-stick or tongue-and-groove sets. The easiest way I've found to check for square is to mount a long (accurate) straightedge on the spindle between two collars and lower the spindle until the straightedge just touches the table, as shown in the left photo above. Of course, both ends of the straightedge should be touching the table at the same time. If this isn't the case, you need to adjust either the table or the spindle assembly with metal shims. Look in the manual for your machine or examine the machine itself to determine the best way to square the spindle.

Next, check the insert rings to see if they are flush with the table surface. To check this, simply place the edge of a straightedge across the rings and the table (see the right photo above). Most insert rings have elevating screws to make any necessary

TUNING THE FENCE

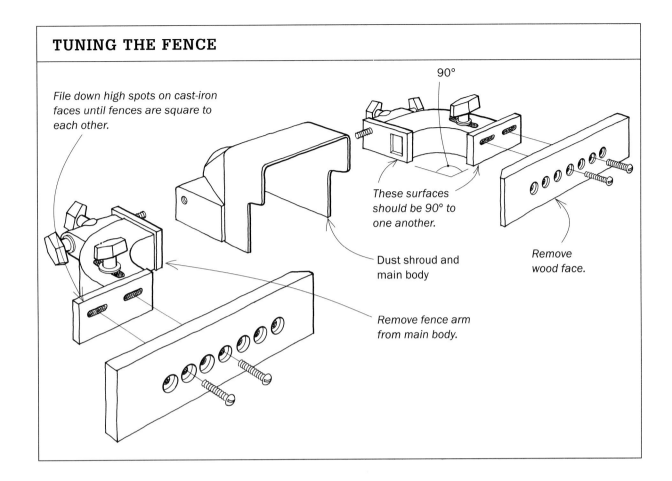

File down high spots on cast-iron faces until fences are square to each other.

90°

These surfaces should be 90° to one another.

Dust shroud and main body

Remove wood face.

Remove fence arm from main body.

adjustments. Having the insert rings flush with the table is critical for good stock support next to the spindle.

Finally, check the split-fence halves with a straightedge. They should be in alignment with each other, but often with new shapers they are not. If they are not in alignment, remove the arms from the main body and remove the wood faces from the arms (see the drawing above). The two machined surfaces on the arm should be 90° to one other. Any problems with alignment are often caused by high spots on the machined surfaces on the fence body or the arm where they attach. You can remedy the problem by smoothing away the offending high spots with a mill file to bring the fence into square.

2

Shaper Cutterheads

No matter how expensive your shaper may be, it is the cutterhead that will ultimately determine the quality of the cut. The cutterhead, or tooling, should be well-balanced, safe to use and sharp enough to produce a wood surface that requires very little sanding. In the past, I've tried cutterheads that vibrated noisily and others that left the wood fibers slightly burned or fuzzy. But those are exceptions now rather than the rule: These days there are a lot of excellent cutterheads to choose from. There are three basic types for use with the shaper—wing cutterheads, insert cutterheads and lockedge knives (see the photos on the facing page). In this chapter, I'll discuss these cutterheads and their applications, plus I'll talk about the types of edge materials available for cutterheads.

Wing Cutterheads

Wing cutterheads are available in a wider variety of profiles and edge materials than ever before. They are machined from solid steel and have two or three wings tipped with carbide or Tantung brand (for more on these and other edge materials, see pp. 30-31). Because there are no knives to set up (or work loose), wing cutterheads are the safest and most convenient of all cutterheads to use. Most wing cutterheads that I've used are extremely well-balanced, which contributes significantly to their safety and

Three types of shaper cutterheads.
From left to right: wing cutterhead,
lockedge knife and insert cutterhead.

Wing cutterheads are available in a wide variety of profiles and edge
materials. They are the safest and most convenient of all cutterheads to use.
On the right is a three-wing cutterhead; on the left a panel-raising cutterhead.

smoothness of cut. However, a big drawback to wing cutterheads is
their cost. A dozen or so cutterheads of various profiles can quickly
add up to the price of a medium-size shaper.

The most recent development in wing cutterheads is a solid-
body, anti-kickback design. Shaper kickbacks are most often caused
by excessively heavy cuts. The solid-body wing cutterheads reduce
the chances of kickback by limiting the amount of wood that can be
removed in a single pass (see the photo on p. 25). Although the
same effect can be achieved with a shaper fence, this built-in
feature adds an extra margin of safety, especially for those with
limited shaper experience.

Collars

Collars are metal rings that mount on the spindle with the cutter-head. Made of solid steel or fitted with ball-bearings, collars are used to control the depth of cut, position the cutterhead high on the spindle or provide spacing between stacked cutterheads. The inside diameter of a collar should be the same size as the spindle on which it is placed. The outside diameter is determined by the desired depth of cut or by the diameter of the cutterhead.

A solid-steel collar is typically used as a spacer between stacked cutterheads. The outside diameter of the collar is the same as the hub diameter of the cutterhead being used. A steel collar can also be positioned below the cutterhead to raise it higher on the spindle when shaping toward the center of wide stock.

A collar fitted with ball bearings is called a rub collar and is used to control the depth of cut when shaping curved stock. The outside diameter of a rub collar is determined by the diameter of the cutterhead and the required depth of cut.

Collars control the depth of cut, position the cutterhead high on the spindle or provide spacing between stacked cutterheads.

A rub collar works the same way as a ball-bearing pilot on a router bit. It rides the edge of the stock to guide the cutterhead and to limit the cutting depth. Although a solid-steel collar may be used for the same purpose, a rub collar will not burn the stock.

The rub collar may be placed above or below the cutterhead, but in most situations it is safer to mount it above the cutterhead and to cut from underneath the stock. This way the stock will act as a barrier between the cutterhead and your hands.

A rub collar controls the depth of cut when shaping curved stock.

COPE-AND-STICK WING CUTTERHEADS

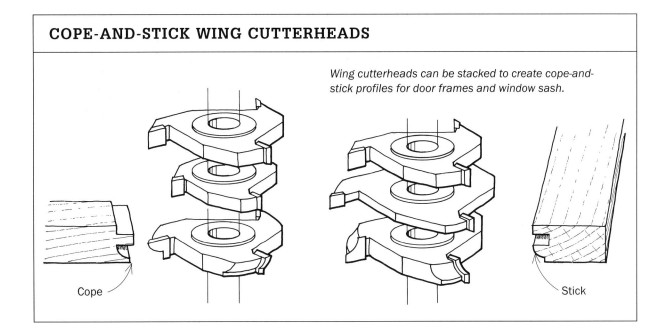

Wing cutterheads can be stacked to create cope-and-stick profiles for door frames and window sash.

Cope

Stick

Most wing cutterheads are designed for shaping both straight and curved stock. But when shaping curved stock, a ball-bearing rub collar must be positioned on the spindle above or below the cutterhead to guide the stock and limit the cutting depth. Be sure to follow the manufacturer's guidelines for using wing cutterheads with curved stock and use the recommended rub collars (for more on collars, see the facing page).

One type of wing cutterhead that has become very popular is the cope-and-stick set (see the drawing above). The cutterheads in this set stack together on the spindle for producing coped doors and sash. One set of cutterheads produces the decorative sticking, and the other set produces the cope. The drawback of cope-and-stick sets is that they produce a very short tenon. So although these sets are useful, I prefer the stub spindle for coping traditional deep mortise-and-tenon joinery. (I've included techniques for coping on the shaper in Chapters 8 and 9.)

A solid-body wing cutterhead (right) reduces the chance of kickback. For the same amount of safety with the old-style cutterhead (left), a fence would have to be used.

Insert Cutterheads

An insert cutterhead (also called insert tooling) uses separate knife sets, which mechanically lock into the head, or body. The head is machined from a chunk of steel or aluminum, and the knives are typically made of high-speed steel (HSS) but may be carbide- or steel-tipped. Knives are available in a wide variety of standard profiles and can be purchased separately or in sets along with the head. An insert cutterhead is a flexible, economical alternative to a set of wing cutterheads: You need only to buy a new pair of knives to add a new profile. Although setting up an insert cutterhead requires some extra time and skill, I find that the dollars saved are often worth it.

The main difference between manufactured insert cutterheads is the method of attaching the knives to the head. Designers have come up with several methods for securing the knives into the head. With one method, serrations on the backs of the knives mesh with serrations in the head (see the left photo below) to hold the knives firmly. Another design, which is very similar to cutterheads in planers and jointers, utilizes pins in the head that slip into holes in the knives (see the right photo below). Pressure from a metal plate, called a gib, maintains the mechanical interlock. Yet another

Insert cutterheads hold knives in the head by way of matching serrations in the knives and the head.

This insert cutterhead set utilizes pins that slip into holes in the knives to hold the knives in the head. Pressure from a gib maintains the interlock.

insert cutterhead secures the knives to the head with screws (see the photo at right). Each knife is drilled and counterbored to accept the screws. This type of knife attachment allows the cutterhead to cut deeper profiles, such as raised panels, because the knives have more support from the head.

Whenever using insert tooling, always read and follow the manufacturer's instructions carefully. Never exceed the maximum rpm specified. Also, most insert cutterheads are not designed to be used freehand, so check with the manufacturer. Failure to follow the manufacturer's instructions could result in serious injury.

The knives for this insert cutterhead are secured to the head with screws.

Lockedge Knives

Another type of cutterhead I use employs a pair of knives secured between disks (called collars). On older setups of this type, the knives had smooth beveled edges, which fit into V-grooves in the collars. However, this system made it fairly easy for the knives to fly out during use if they were not in tight. Manufacturers improved the system by replacing the smooth-edge knives with lockedge knives, which virtually eliminated the possibility of a thrown knife (see the photo on p. 28).

One edge of each knife is serrated to mate with a worm screw in the collar. The collars are then fastened together with machine screws. The whole system—knives, collars and screws—is then placed on the shaper spindle. For an additional cost, the collars may be ordered with a ball-bearing ring for use as a rub collar for shaping curved work.

Although I own several types of cutterheads, I prefer the lockedge knives for several reasons. By far the biggest advantage is that I can grind custom profiles. This gives me enormous flexibility that other cutterheads cannot provide. Although learning to grind the steel and to create fluid curves takes a bit of practice, it's not terribly difficult (see Chapter 7). Lockedge knives are also very economical. On average, I can make several profiles for the cost of just one wing cutterhead. And unlike ball-bearing router bits and shaper cutterheads, when the knives become shortened on this system, they can be extended from the collar to maintain the proper cutting depth.

A lockedge knife is serrated, and the collar engages the serrations to hold the knife fast. The collars are tightened with hex-head screws.

Even though the ordinary smooth-edge steel system is still available, I highly recommend the lockedge system because it's safer and works just as well. With either system, be sure to follow all steps and precautions outlined by the tooling manufacturer when setting up the cutterheads.

Custom-Made Cutterheads

If you occasionally need an unusual profile, you might consider using a lockedge cutterhead and grinding the knife profile yourself. It's not a difficult skill to learn, and it gives you enormous shaping flexibility. If you're not comfortable with grinding the profile yourself, another choice is to have the cutterhead custom-made. Most tooling manufacturers offer custom tooling for wing cutterheads, insert cutterheads and bevel-edge knives in HSS or edged with Tantung or carbide.

Although custom tooling isn't inexpensive, depending on the profile, it often doesn't cost much more than stock cutterheads. To

Custom profiles can be ground into lockedge knife stock (top). The stock locks into the collars (bottom).

order a custom cutterhead, you must send the manufacturer a list of information, including a drawing or sample of the profile, the edge material desired, the bore size and the spindle rotation.

What Type to Buy

Deciding which cutterheads to buy, and which are best for your situation, may be puzzling. In my shop I have several types of cutterheads of various profiles. A good starting point would be Tantung-tipped wing cutterheads. I like these cutterheads for their convenience and for the smooth finished surface they create on natural wood. If you'll be making a wide variety of profiles, I'd suggest extending your tooling budget to include an insert cutterhead set. Because I frequently need to reproduce old profiles or make custom profiles, I have quite a large collection of lockedge knives that I've ground myself; and I also keep a supply of carbide-tipped wing cutterheads in several standard shapes for shaping the more abrasive, man-made materials.

Edge Materials for Shaper Cutterheads

When buying cutterheads for your shaper, an important consideration is the material used to make the cutting edge. In general, shaper cutterheads are made from high-speed steel (used most often for insert cutterheads), or they are tipped with carbide or Tantung. You should know a bit about these materials and which works best for a particular cutting job. The edge materials will play an important part in your choice of cutterheads (along with cost).

High-speed steel

High-speed steel (HSS) has been used for shaper cutterheads for many years in a wide variety of applications. However, these days HSS has been replaced on most wing cutterheads by newer, longer-wearing edge materials, such as carbide and Tantung. But HSS is still advantageous as insert tooling. Because it's inexpensive and easily ground to profile, HSS is often the best choice for short production runs of custom profiles. Also, because HSS can be sharpened to a finer edge than carbide, it is particularly suitable for creating a surface on hardwoods that is smooth and free of the burn marks sometimes associated with carbide-edge cutterheads.

Carbide

The advantages of carbide-edge tools are well-known. Because it is extremely hard, carbide retains its cutting edge for extensive periods, which means your cutterheads spend less time at a sharpening shop. Because of its resistance to wear, carbide is by far the best edge material for shaping man-made materials, such as medium-density fiberboard (MDF) or plywood, or any natural wood that has been glued up into larger stock.

Carbide is a mixture of metal powder and a binder material molded at extreme pressure and temperature. The quality of carbide can vary considerably, however, so it's helpful to have a basic knowledge of its characteristics when comparing cutterheads.

Carbide is brazed onto the steel body of the cutterhead or locked in mechanically (it is typically brazed onto the tips of wing cutterheads). As the carbide dulls, the granular structure breaks away. High-quality carbide has a fine, uniform granular structure that wears slowly and evenly. In contrast, poor-quality carbide is made of large, uneven particles that break down quickly and unevenly. So although it may cost less initially, inexpensive carbide tooling can end up costing more in the long run because of the short life of the cutterhead and the added expense of frequent sharpening.

Of course it is impossible to determine carbide grain size

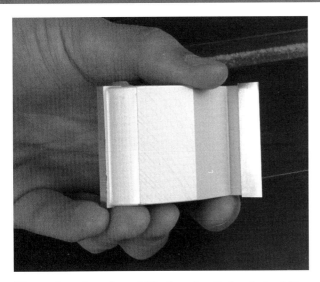

The cutting edge of a carbide-tipped cutterhead should be polished and free of sharpening marks.

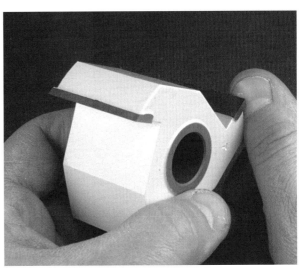

A good, sharp edge will shave the surface of your thumbnail (use a light touch).

without magnification, but there are a few things you can look for when comparing carbide cutterheads. First, examine the cutting edge for finish quality. The surface should be polished and free of coarse grinding marks from sharpening. Also, check the edge for sharpness by carefully shaving the surface of your thumbnail. Finally, when examining wing cutterheads, compare the thickness of the carbide tips. Although it costs a bit more, thicker carbide generally means a longer tool life.

Tantung

Tantung, a trade name for S-alloy, is an edge material with the durability of carbide and the sharpness of HSS. Like carbide, Tantung is used for tips on wing cutterheads. Because of Tantung's durability and sharpness, cutterheads with this edge material leave a smooth finished surface on natural wood that requires very little sanding. But when it comes to shaping man-made materials, Tantung, although more wear-resistant than HSS, is not as wear-resistant as carbide. So for these materials, carbide-tipped cutterheads are still the best choice.

3

Shaper Safety

I clearly remember the large, gray shaper in my high-school woodworking class. It sat idle in a far corner of the shop gathering wood dust generated by the other machines. As students, we were told very little about the shaper—only that it was too dangerous to use and that all shaping would be done with a table-mounted router. However, the shaper can be both productive *and* safe. The key to safe shaper use is understanding how the shaper operates and approaching the shaper each and every time with a keen awareness of its inherent dangers. To use the shaper without getting hurt, you'll need to employ both common sense and the appropriate safety devices.

Safety Devices

Over the years, several types of safety devices have been developed for use with the shaper. Some devices prevent chatter and kickback, while others provide a barrier between your hands and the cutterhead. Some devices, such as push blocks, are common safety accessories that you may already own. Other devices can be purchased from shaper manufacturers, and some you can even make in your shop.

Because using the shaper often involves complex or unusual setups, you may not be able to guard yourself with only the safety devices supplied by the manufacturer. It's important to work as safely as possible, so if the manufacturer's guards won't work, then use an aftermarket safety device or design and build one of your own. What follows is a list of devices that I use to increase shaper safety in my own shop and in the university woodworking shop where I teach.

FENCES

When properly adjusted, a standard, manufacturer-supplied fence surrounds the cutterhead and shields your hands. But the standard fence is not always best-suited for custom work. If you build a special fence for an unusual job, make sure that the fence surrounds the cutterhead as much as possible so that it protects you and supports the stock sufficiently. And always make sure that any fence is secured to the table before starting the machine.

When using large-diameter cutterheads, such as those for panel-raising, I prefer a margin of safety beyond what is provided by the standard fence. I use a box fence, which completely surrounds the cutterhead (see p. 17). The box fence provides a solid barrier between my hands and the cutterhead and is easily made in the shop. (For information on building other custom fences, see Chapter 1.)

Always wear safety glasses and ear protection and try to keep your hands 6 in. from the cutterhead.

INSERT RINGS

Insert rings are graduated, interlocking rings that fit in the shaper table around the spindle (see the drawing on p. 19). They are installed or removed to accommodate different-size cutterheads and support the stock to maintain accuracy during shaping. But the rings also help avoid kickback by preventing narrow stock from dropping into the opening around the spindle. As a general rule, always keep the opening around the spindle as small as possible.

GUARDS

It's important to use a guard to provide a barrier between your hands and the spinning cutterhead, particularly when shaping curved stock. One such guard is a ring guard, which is a metal ring suspended over the cutterhead with an arm (see the left photo on p. 34). This simple device is mounted out of the way on the back edge of the shaper table. This type of guard is offered as an accessory by most shaper manufacturers and is usually 3½ in. in diameter.

When you'll be shaping curved stock with a cutterhead that exceeds 3½ in. in diameter, you can use a similar device called the Safe Guard II (see the right photo on p. 34). The Safe Guard II is a

Guards are designed to protect your hands while shaping. The ring guard (left) is suspended over the cutterhead. The Safe Guard II (right) mounts on the spindle, above the cutterhead, and can be used with the shaper fence.

transparent plastic disk that mounts directly on the spindle, above the cutterhead. Designed and manufactured by Delta, the disk can also be used in conjunction with the shaper fence (but I find it most effective for shaping curved stock). The Safe Guard II is available in either 4½-in. or 6½-in. diameters for spindle sizes ranging from ½ in. to 1¼ in.

FEATHERBOARDS

Featherboards are important safety devices for the shaper. They prevent chatter and reduce the likelihood of kickback by holding the stock firmly against the fence and the table. They are most effective on narrow stock. Featherboards may be purchased as aftermarket safety devices (see the photo on the facing page), or you can make your own out of wood (a typical design is shown in the drawing on the facing page).

Each "finger" of the featherboard works as a small spring to push the stock against the table or fence. To make a featherboard, use a hardwood plank approximately 1¼ in. by 6 in. by 16 in. Cut one end of the plank to 30° and make the fingers approximately 5 in. long and ⅛ in. wide. (I cut the fingers with a wide blade on the bandsaw.) To use the featherboard, clamp it to the shaper top so that the space between the fingers of the featherboard and the fence is slightly less than the width of the stock.

MAKING AND USING A FEATHERBOARD

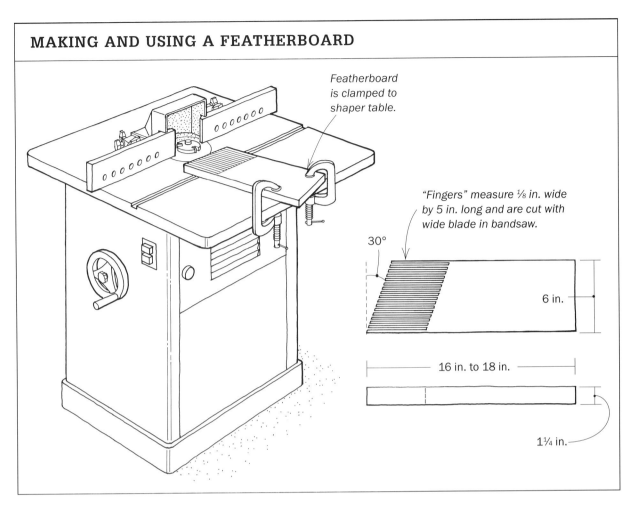

Featherboard
is clamped to
shaper table.

"Fingers" measure ⅛ in. wide
by 5 in. long and are cut with
wide blade in bandsaw.

30°

6 in.

16 in. to 18 in.

1¼ in.

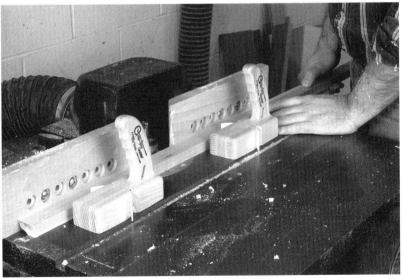

These magnetic featherboards hold stock tightly against the fence, reduce chatter and help prevent kickback.

Push blocks keep your hands away from the spinning cutterhead.

PUSH BLOCKS, SAFETY GLASSES AND EAR PROTECTION

Three of the main safety devices used with a shaper are probably (or at least should be) mainstays of your shop arsenal already: push blocks, safety glasses and ear protection. Push blocks allow you to keep a safe distance between your hands and the whirling cutterhead—they're especially important when shaping narrow stock (see the photo above). (As a rule, always keep your hands at least 6 in. from the cutterhead.)

Eye and ear protection is a must for working with any woodworking machine. But they're especially important with the shaper. The shaper is loud, and I'd recommend using proven ear protection (simple ear plugs may not be sufficient). And because the shaper cutterhead is often exposed partially or fully, bits of wood and shavings are hurled everywhere. So wear safety glasses at all times.

Preventing Kickbacks

Just like a table saw, a shaper can kick back with incredible violence and speed. Kickbacks are extremely hazardous for two reasons: You could be struck by the material as it is kicked back, and/or your hands can be pulled into the cutterhead. The key is to understand the causes of kickback and the necessary precautions to prevent them. What follows are a few simple tips that can help you avoid kickback while using your shaper.

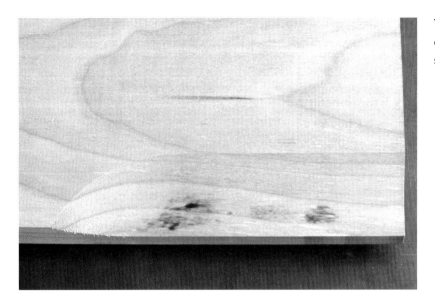

When the cutterhead starts to burn or glaze the wood, it's time to sharpen it.

USE SHARP CUTTERHEADS

Rather than shearing off the wood fibers, a dull cutterhead "beats" the stock, which could cause kickback. When a cutterhead starts to burn or glaze the wood (see the photo above), create an unusual amount of feed resistance or climb the stock (when the cutterhead partially rides over the stock), it is past time for sharpening. Before using a cutterhead, always examine its cutting edges for wear. A sharp cutterhead will shave your fingernail. The edges should be polished to a uniform sheen and free of small nicks. For close examination, I use a 10x magnifying glass.

TAKE LIGHT CUTS

One of the most common causes of kickback is taking too heavy a cut. Setting up the shaper for an excessively heavy cut causes each knife to take a large bite out of the stock. This in turn causes chatter and kickback. The maximum safe depth of the cut is determined by the size and density of the stock, the horsepower of the shaper and the size of the edge profile. Always start by taking light cuts (about ⅛ in.) until you get a feel for what is safe. Experience is the key here.

Shape oversized stock, then trim it to size. To help prevent kickbacks, avoid shaping narrow or small stock.

SHAPE LARGE STOCK, THEN TRIM IT

Kickbacks with small stock are often the most dangerous. Avoid shaping narrow, thin or short stock. Instead, shape oversized stock and reduce it to size after shaping (see the photo above). If this is not possible, use some sort of jig or a featherboard to hold the stock against the fence and the table. Also, keep the cut light and the fence opening small. It may even be necessary to use a zero-clearance fence (see the photo on p. 18).

PROVIDE SUFFICIENT SUPPORT FOR STOCK

To avoid kickbacks, it's important to adjust the spindle and fence openings appropriately for the size of the stock to be shaped. If the fence or spindle opening is larger than the stock, it will drop into the cutterhead and cause a kickback. Use the insert rings around the spindle and adjust the fence for the smallest possible opening that allows the profile to be shaped. When shaping curved stock freehand, it must be braced against the starting pin upon entering the cutterhead. Attempting to shape stock freehand without a starting pin is an invitation for kickback.

Safety Guidelines

• For most cuts, feed the stock against the rotation of the cutterhead (it is acceptable and sometimes desirable to feed the stock in the direction of the cutterhead, but only with a power feeder). If your machine has a reversing switch, check the spindle rotation before feeding the stock to prevent your hands from being pulled into the cutterhead.

• Select a speed appropriate for the diameter of the cutterhead. Large cutterheads have faster rim speeds than small cutterheads when run at the same rpm and so should be run at a lower rpm than small cutterheads. Check with the cutterhead manufacturer for maximum rpm of a specific cutterhead.

• Always use a keyed lockwasher to prevent the locknut from backing off the spindle.

• Don't run large cutterheads on small spindles, even if you have the bushings to do it. Small spindles are not designed to handle the forces exerted by large cutterheads.

• Whenever possible, position the cutterhead so that it cuts from

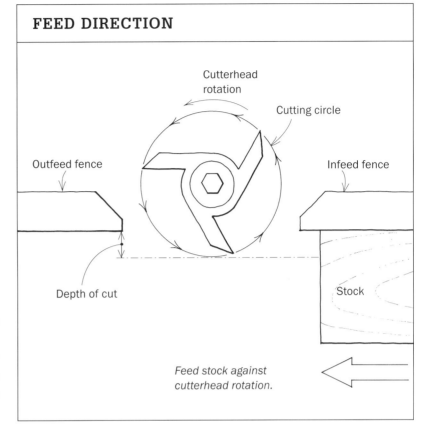

FEED DIRECTION

Cutterhead rotation

Cutting circle

Outfeed fence

Infeed fence

Depth of cut

Stock

Feed stock against cutterhead rotation.

underneath the stock. This way, the stock acts as a guard, and the portion of the cutterhead not being used is below the table surface.

• Always use guards. If the guard that came with your machine can't be used for a given operation, buy an accessory guard or make one.

• Keep your hands a minimum of 6 in. from the cutterhead when

the shaper is running. If necessary, use push blocks to keep your hands away.

• Wear ear and eye protection.

• Unplug the shaper before making setups or adjustments.

• Always use sound judgment and common sense. Double-check every setup and ask yourself, "Is this setup safe?" If you don't feel comfortable, don't try it.

4

Basic Shaper Technique

A three-wing cutterhead is the easiest to set up and the safest to use. Mount it to cut from underneath the stock.

The most basic use of a shaper is to produce a molding profile on the edge of straight stock. Because of its simplicity, this job is a good place to start learning about shaping, yet it involves many of the same techniques used for advanced cuts. These include setting up the shaper, shaping an entire edge, shaping end grain and creating stop cuts.

Setting Up the Shaper

Regardless of the type of cut you're going to make, there are five main steps to setting up the shaper: Mount the cutterhead, adjust the spindle height, align the fence, secure the guard and make a test cut. I'd suggest you begin by selecting a small, three-wing cutterhead with a simple profile, such as a bead or ogee (for more on cutterheads, see Chapter 2). A three-wing cutterhead is relatively safe to use and easy to set up (see the photo at left). Mount it so that it will cut from underneath the stock rather than on top of the stock. (Cutting from underneath is safer because the stock shields your hands from the cutterhead.)

If the cutterhead that you've selected is designed to cut from on top of the stock, you can turn the cutterhead over, reverse the spindle rotation and cut from the opposite direction. Remember, always cut against the rotation of the spindle to prevent the stock

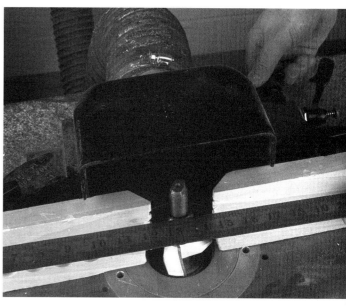

Gauge the spindle height by placing a sample molding next to the cutterhead.

Use a long straightedge to help align the fence halves.

from pulling out of your hands and to prevent your hands from being pulled into the cutterhead. If possible, mount the cutterhead on the lower half of the spindle, which will reduce wear on the spindle bearings. Secure the cutterhead with the locknut and the keyed washer. Then rotate the spindle by hand to see that the cutterhead clears the table opening and the fence.

Now adjust the spindle height with the handwheel. If you have a sample molding, place it next to the cutterhead to set the height exactly (see the left photo above), then lock the spindle in position. If you don't have a sample molding available, use a machinist's rule with fine graduations to gauge the distance between the cutterhead and the table surface.

The next step is to align the fence. Because the fence guides the stock and controls the depth of cut, it must be accurately positioned in relationship to the cutterhead. First, use the micrometer knob to adjust the offset in the fence halves. Make certain that the two halves are in the same plane with the help of a long straightedge (see the right photo above). Then position the fence on the shaper table to expose just enough of the cutterhead to shape the complete profile and tighten the nuts that secure the fence to the table. Again, rotate the cutterhead by hand to make sure that it clears the fence and the table insert (see the photo at right). Remember to keep the size of the fence opening as small as possible to support the stock and prevent it from tipping

Rotate the cutterhead by hand to make sure it clears the table insert and the fence.

dangerously into the cutterhead. Also, now's the time to secure the guard to the fence. Finally, set the spindle for a low speed.

Once all the adjustments have been made, take a test cut. I always shape an inch or two on a test piece of the same thickness as the actual stock. Then I check the profile against a drawing or an existing molding and readjust the shaper as necessary.

Feed rate is important to achieve a smooth surface on the finished stock. Feeding the stock too fast will produce a rippled, washboard surface because each knife is taking a large cut. Too slow a feed rate may cause a burned or glazed surface, which results from excess friction as the knives continually rub the stock.

Shaping an Entire Edge

Some cutterhead profiles are designed to remove the entire edge of the stock, such as a radius edge of a tabletop (see the drawing below). The edge-profile example I'm using here is based upon the cyma curve and is found on Queen Anne furniture, such as dressing tables or lowboys. Because the profile can't be found in shaper-tooling catalogs, I chose to grind the profile myself using high-speed steel (HSS) lockedge cutters (for more on grinding custom cutterheads, see Chapter 7).

To allow for shaping of an entire edge, I mill the stock $1/32$ in. longer than its finished length. This way I can remove $1/64$ in. from each end and create a flowing profile. I leave the stock about $1/4$ in.

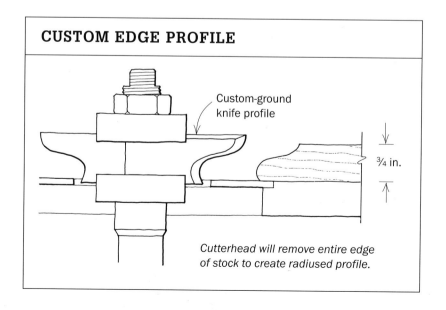

CUSTOM EDGE PROFILE

Custom-ground knife profile

3/4 in.

Cutterhead will remove entire edge of stock to create radiused profile.

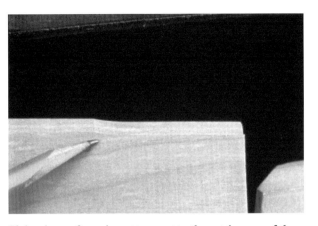

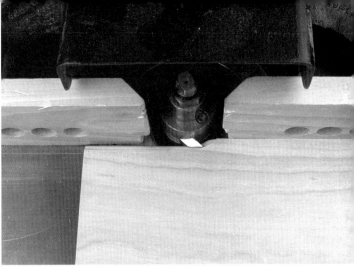

If the shaper fence is not tangent to the cutting arc of the cutterhead, the result will be an end snipe.

Shape a test piece until it reaches the outfeed fence. With the shaper off, move the outfeed fence forward until it just makes contact with the stock. Then lock it in place.

to ½ in. wider than its finished size as well. In the case of this tabletop, I've left it ½ in. wide. Because the back edge of the tabletop traditionally isn't molded, I'll rip the top to final width after shaping. This technique will remove minor tearout, or splintering, on the trailing edge of the cut as a result of shaping.

Begin by mounting the cutterhead and adjusting the spindle height. Set the fence so that just enough wood will be removed from the stock to fully shape the profile. (Removing more stock than necessary is wasteful, creates more work for the machine and requires greater feed pressure.) When shaping an entire edge, like the edge of this tabletop, the stock will be end-sniped (slightly reduced in width) after it passes the cutterhead (see the left photo above). To prevent the stock from being end-sniped, you must bring the outfeed fence slightly forward of the infeed fence to support the stock. In other words, the outfeed fence must be tangent to the cutting arc of the cutterhead.

This is an exact adjustment made with the help of a test piece. Turn on the power and shape enough stock to reach the outfeed fence—the first 3 in. or 4 in. is usually sufficient. With the power turned off, carefully move the outfeed fence forward until it just makes contact with the stock (see the right photo above), then lock the outfeed fence. Now shape the entire length of the test piece. If the trailing end is sniped, the outfeed fence needs to come forward a bit more. Turn off the shaper, readjust the fence and then make another test cut. When the split fence is properly adjusted, the stock will be straight with no end snipe.

Shaping End Grain

Shaping end grain creates special problems. End grain is tough and will burn easily, so cutterheads should be kept very sharp. But a bigger problem is the tearout that results when the trailing edge of the stock passes the cutterhead, causing splintering and chipout. Fortunately, there are several methods to eliminate the problems encountered on end grain.

The simplest solution is to shape the end grain of the stock first (see the drawing below) and then shape the edges. Shaping the edges after the end grain removes the tearout near the trailing edge. I often shape raised panels with this method.

An alternative method is to position a backup board behind the stock to support the trailing edge. The backup board can be fastened to the miter gauge (see the photo on the facing page), and this method is especially effective for shaping the end grain of narrow stock. Another simple solution is to start with oversize stock

SHAPING END GRAIN

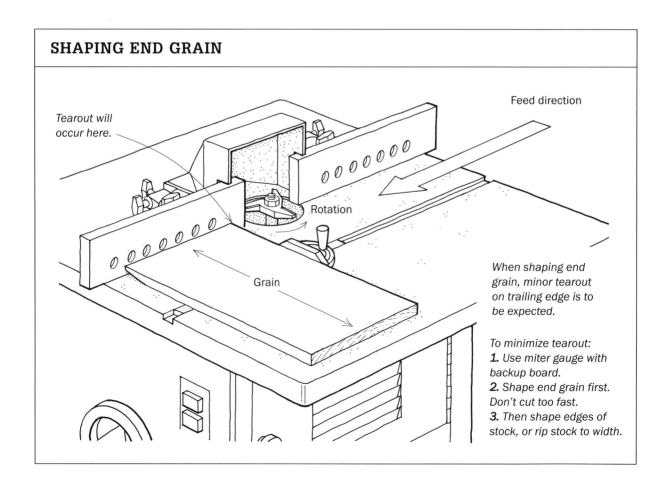

Tearout will occur here.

Feed direction

Rotation

Grain

When shaping end grain, minor tearout on trailing edge is to be expected.

To minimize tearout:
1. Use miter gauge with backup board.
2. Shape end grain first. Don't cut too fast.
3. Then shape edges of stock, or rip stock to width.

To eliminate tearout on the trailing edge when shaping end grain, attach a backup board to the miter gauge to provide support. This method is especially effective for shaping the end grain of narrow stock.

and then to rip it to final width after shaping. This is an effective way to remove end-grain tearout when the edges of the stock will not have a shaped profile.

Creating Stop Cuts

For decorative purposes, a shaped profile will sometimes begin and/or end somewhere in the middle of a piece of stock. This is referred to as a stop cut, and it is made by plunging the stock into the spinning cutterhead. To produce a stop cut safely and accurately, stop blocks should be clamped to the shaper fence to limit the cut and to prevent kickback. Also, the cut should be small in comparison to the workpiece. Experience is important, so start with small cuts.

An example of a stop cut is a stop chamfer (see the drawing at right), which softens the hard edges of a piece and adds a

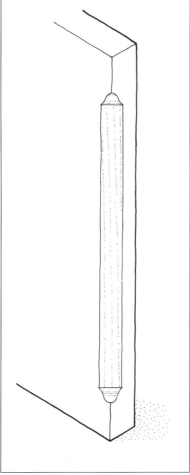

STOP CUT

Stop chamfer can be created on shaper with a 45° cutterhead. Ogee profile at ends of chamfer are carved by hand.

decorative touch. After shaping, I hand-carve the ogee profile into the ends of the chamfers using chisels and files.

To make a stop cut, begin by marking the stock to indicate where the cut will begin and end (see the photo below). Next, set up the cutterhead so that it cuts from underneath the stock and adjust the fence and spindle for the correct depth of cut. Use a clamp or a stop block to position the stock against the infeed fence for the beginning of the cut (see the top photo on the facing page). The stop block will also prevent the stock from being grabbed and thrown backward as you begin the cut. Make a test cut and readjust the shaper spindle and fence if necessary.

With the shaper running, rest one end of the stock against the stop block and slowly pivot the stock into the spinning cutterhead (see the bottom photo on the facing page). Using the layout lines, advance the stock until you reach the end of the shaped profile. When I'm shaping multiple pieces, I also clamp a stock block to the outfeed fence to guarantee uniformity. A second stop block also increases efficiency because you don't have to search for the stopping point while shaping.

Mark on the workpiece where the stop cut begins and ends.

Use a clamp or a stop block to position the workpiece for the beginning of the cut.

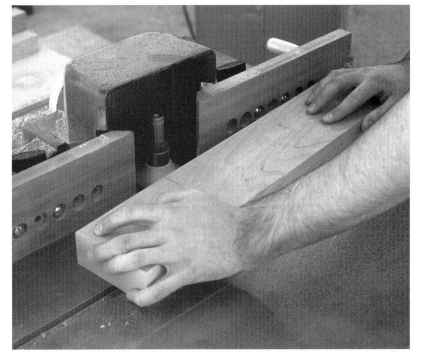

With the shaper running, rest one end of the stock against the stop and slowly pivot the stock into the cutterhead.

5

Shaping Curved Stock

Learning to shape curved stock opens a whole new realm of woodworking possibilities. No longer must you be limited to building furniture of constant rectilinear form. Many styles of furniture and architecture contain curvilinear forms, including my favorite, Queen Anne. Even if you build contemporary furniture that has few, if any, classic molding profiles, you can still use the shaper to remove the bandsaw marks quickly from curved surfaces.

Curved stock is shaped one of three ways. Each way provides a different method of controlling the cut. The first method, often referred to as freehand shaping, uses the edge of the stock as a reference point. A ball-bearing rub collar rides against the edge and limits the cut. This can only be done when you're shaping a portion of the edge. To shape the entire edge, you'll need to use a pattern in conjunction with the rub collar. The third method allows you to shape the *face* of the stock. The control for the cut is provided by a shop-built jig that attaches to the fence of the shaper.

Before beginning, it's important to note that shaping curved stock is where accidents often occur. The procedures in this chapter are inherently dangerous, and you should only attempt them after you've gained plenty of experience shaping straight stock. All safety rules for shaping curved work must be followed, including the use of a ring guard (for more on shaper safety, see Chapter 3).

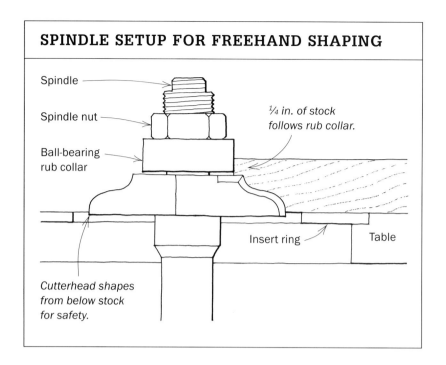

SPINDLE SETUP FOR FREEHAND SHAPING

Spindle

Spindle nut

Ball-bearing rub collar

¼ in. of stock follows rub collar.

Insert ring

Table

Cutterhead shapes from below stock for safety.

Shaping Freehand

The simplest method of shaping a profile on the inside or outside radius edge of curved stock is to do it freehand. Freehand shaping doesn't require that you make a jig or pattern. However, you can only use this method for profiles in which only part of the edge will be shaped because you'll need to leave at least ¼ in. of the edge thickness to ride against the rub collar (see the drawing at right). Because the stock edge guides the cutterhead, the edge must be free of bandsaw marks and surface irregularities. The drawing above shows a typical spindle arrangement for freehand shaping. (Although freehand shaping is simple, it's still a good idea to make a few practice runs with the shaper turned off.)

To prevent the stock from kicking back as you enter the cut, use a starting pin. The starting pin, which is a tapered steel rod inserted in the table, is used as a fulcrum to pivot the stock into the cutterhead. The pin must be on the thrust side of the cutterhead so that you will be cutting *against* the rotation of the spindle (see the drawing on p. 50).

Most important, the stock must be of sufficient size to prevent chatter and to allow the placement of your hands a safe distance from the cutterhead (6 in. minimum). I recommend leaving the

PROFILES THAT MAY BE SHAPED FREEHAND

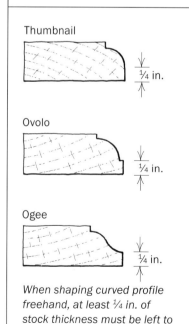

Thumbnail

¼ in.

Ovolo

¼ in.

Ogee

¼ in.

When shaping curved profile freehand, at least ¼ in. of stock thickness must be left to ride against rub collar.

FREEHAND SHAPING

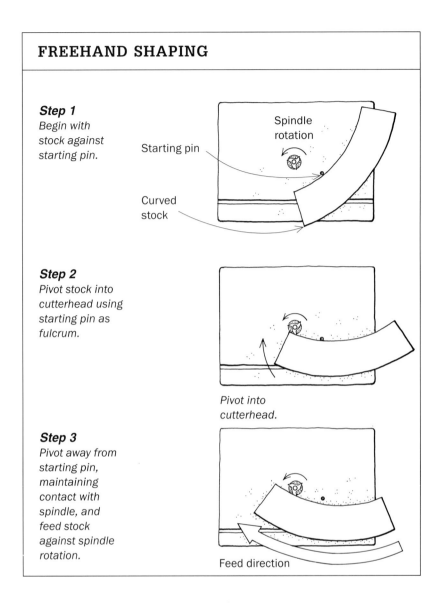

Step 1
Begin with stock against starting pin.

Spindle rotation

Starting pin

Curved stock

Step 2
Pivot stock into cutterhead using starting pin as fulcrum.

Pivot into cutterhead.

Step 3
Pivot away from starting pin, maintaining contact with spindle, and feed stock against spindle rotation.

Feed direction

stock larger than its final dimensions to provide safe hand placement. The stock can then be reduced to final dimension after it is safely shaped. The drawing above shows the steps to freehand shaping.

As an example of freehand shaping, I'm going to use the rear leg of a Queen Anne chair. The lower portion of the leg is chamfered on all four corners. The chamfer is ⁹⁄₁₆ in. wide and stops 1 in. below the seat rail. This is a light cut on a long piece of stock—a good example for someone who wants to try freehand shaping of curved stock for the first time.

For shaping freehand, begin by mounting the cutterhead on the spindle so that it cuts from underneath the stock.

Mount a ball-bearing rub collar above the cutterhead. Put on the ring guard and the keyed lockwasher, tighten the spindle nut and insert the starting pin.

To begin, mount a three-wing chamfer cutterhead on the spindle (see the left photo on the facing page) so that it cuts from underneath the stock. This positions most of the cutterhead safely below the surface of the shaper table (you'll need to remove a couple of insert rings around the spindle to do this). Next, mount a ball-bearing rub collar (see the right photo above) above the cutterhead. Position a ring guard above the rub collar, then slip on the keyed lockwasher (ring guard is removed in photos for clarity). Finally, tighten the spindle nut securely.

Next, insert the starting pin so that the stock can be fed against the spindle rotation (see the drawing on the facing page). If the spindle rotation is counterclockwise, the pin will be on the right. If it is clockwise, the pin will be on the left. Also, double-check the spindle rotation to make sure that it is indeed rotating in the correct direction. Remember, too, that before shaping the profile, the surface of the stock must be a smooth, fair curve. Finally, use the handwheel to adjust the cutterhead height and lock it into position.

To begin shaping, position the stock against the starting pin. Pivot the stock slowly and carefully into the spinning cutterhead until it contacts the rub collar at a point tangent to the collar surface. Once the stock contacts the rub collar, immediately begin feeding the stock forward and simultaneously pivot it away from the starting pin. When you've reached the layout line that indicates the stopping point of the cut, simply pull the stock away from the cutterhead. If at any time the stock inadvertently leaves the rub collar, reposition the stock on the starting pin and begin again. Attempting to reenter the cutterhead without the aid of a starting pin is an open invitation for kickback.

When shaping toward the end of the stock, pivot the stock into the cutterhead and aim for the layout line (ring guard has been removed for clarity).

As I've mentioned before, hand position is very important when freehand shaping. You must keep your hands a minimum of 6 in. from the cutterhead—more than that if the cut is large. Begin with both hands behind the cutterhead. Once the leading end of the stock is a safe distance beyond the cutterhead, you may reposition your leading hand. Remember to keep downward pressure on the table. As the stock continues forward through the cut, you must reposition your other hand forward of the cut and pull the stock through the cut with both hands.

If the leg in my example was made from straight stock, the stop cut on all four corners could be shaped in the same direction. However, this leg is curved on two faces, so you'll have to reverse the cutting direction to make the stop cut correctly, starting in the middle of the leg and working toward the foot. That means you'll shape one corner, flip the stock to shape the opposite corner and then reverse the cutting direction to shape the other corners in the same manner. The technique is basically the same as before. When you start to pivot the stock into the cutterhead, aim for the layout

Safety Checklist for Shaping Freehand

- Make sure the stock is large enough to prevent chatter and to provide safe positioning of your hands.

- Check to see that at least ¼ in. of stock thickness is rubbing against the collar.

- Use a ring guard.

- Make sure the starting pin is in place.

- Cut from underneath the stock.

- Feed the stock against the cutterhead rotation.

- Take the cut in two or more passes by using a large rub collar or by lowering the spindle height.

line on the stock (see the photo above). If you come up shy of the layout line, *don't back up*. Instead, pull the stock away and begin again from the starting pin. As the profile reaches the end of the stock, simply pull the stock straight away from the cutterhead. Be careful not to shape the end grain. (A safety checklist for freehand shaping is given above.)

Shaping with a Pattern

Shaping with a pattern is the most efficient and accurate method for shaping curved stock. The pattern controls the depth of cut, and it is also the only way to shape the entire edge of curved parts, such as the profiles shown in the drawing at right. Without the pattern, the stock would be consumed by the cutterhead. The stock is secured to a pattern, or template, of the curved piece, which rides against the rub collar on the spindle (the spindle setup is shown in the drawing on p. 54). You can either put the pattern on top of the stock or on the bottom, but cutting from underneath with the pattern on top is safer because the pattern will shield your hands. A starting pin must be used unless the pattern extends beyond the stock and contacts the rub collar before the stock contacts the cutterhead.

There are two benefits to using a pattern for shaping curved stock. First, each piece is identical. But the bigger benefit by far is the time saved when using this technique, which makes a pattern especially useful for production work. Because the pattern rubs

FULL-EDGE PROFILES REQUIRE A PATTERN

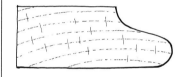

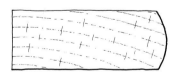

When shaping full-edge profiles like these, attach stock to pattern to provide reference surface.

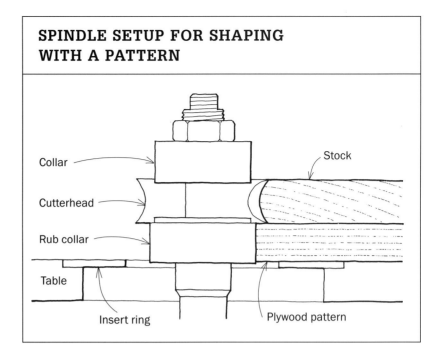

SPINDLE SETUP FOR SHAPING WITH A PATTERN

Collar

Cutterhead

Rub collar

Table

Insert ring

Stock

Plywood pattern

the collar, and the entire edge of the stock is shaped, there is no need to be meticulous about removing the bandsaw marks from the stock prior to shaping. Instead, the stock is sawn slightly oversize, and the cutterhead removes the irregularities as the collar follows the pattern.

The pattern should be made of a high-quality plywood or medium-density fiberboard (MDF) and carefully sawn and sanded smooth. Any bumps or irregularities will be transferred or even magnified in the shaped profile on the stock. The pattern must also allow quick and easy securing and removal of stock for shaping.

I use toggle clamps to hold the stock down on the pattern. To prevent the stock from moving laterally during shaping, I fasten blocks or strips of plywood to the pattern at several locations to counteract the thrust of the cutterhead. Another option is to glue strips of sandpaper to the pattern to hold the stock. Or you can drive small brads into the pattern from underneath and allow the points to protrude $\frac{1}{16}$ in. or so to catch the stock. Position the brads so that the points hit waste areas in the stock or areas that will later be covered by hardware.

On this pattern, the stock is held fast by toggle clamps on top, a stop block at back and small brads driven from underneath the pattern.

A PATTERN FOR SHAPING STOCK WITH ONE CURVED EDGE

A typical pattern used for shaping an entire edge of curved stock is shown in the photo above. The stock in this case is a hinged leaf for an elliptical table. The leaf will later have a pair of hinges mortised into the straight edge and a handle cutout at the apex of the curve. In this case the stock is held fast by toggle clamps on top, a stop block at back and small brads driven from underneath the pattern (the brads were located at the hinge areas and at the cutout area). The pattern for the table leaf extends beyond the stock, so there's no need for a starting pin. Making the pattern slightly larger than the stock is actually somewhat safer than using a starting pin because there is less tendency for the cutterhead to grab as you enter the cut.

Safety is always the most important consideration, regardless of the shaping operation. To prevent kickback, avoid taking excessively heavy cuts. To limit the cutting depth when shaping against a rub collar, use a large-diameter collar first, then switch to a smaller-diameter collar for the final pass.

When shaping curved stock, the smoothest possible surface is achieved by cutting with the grain, sometimes referred to as cutting "downhill." This same principle is applied throughout

When shaping a curved profile, use a sharp cutterhead, take a light cut and feed the work slowly. A starting pin isn't needed because the pattern extends beyond the stock.

woodworking with both hand and power tools. Large woodworking plants and even some custom shops use double-spindle shapers to allow downhill shaping of curved stock. The spindles each have the same cutterhead profiles installed, but they rotate in opposite directions to allow for shaping downhill. The double spindle allows you to change cutting direction easily when the grain direction changes.

Most of us don't have the money or space for a double-spindle machine, so we must exercise other options, one of which is to make two separate setups by reversing the spindle direction. Depending on the cutter profile, it may be possible simply to invert the cutterhead. However, if the profile is asymmetrical, you will need a pair of cutters with the same profile, each designed to run the opposite direction of the other.

Another option is simply to shape the profile the same direction for the entire length of the stock, regardless of the grain direction (see the photo at left). The key to a smooth cut is to use a sharp cutterhead, take a light cut and feed the work slowly. Depending on the density and structure of the wood and the tightness of the curve, tearout can usually be avoided.

A PATTERN FOR SHAPING STOCK WITH TWO CURVED EDGES

With most pattern shaping, the stock has one or more straight edges to reference into the pattern. This makes designing and constructing the pattern relatively straightforward. Sometimes, however, the stock has no straight edges to reference, and a pattern must be constructed to allow referencing of curved surfaces. The rear leg of an 18th-century Queen Anne bow back chair is a good example. Usually, several legs are bandsawed from one wide plank, then the saw marks are removed.

I have removed saw marks by hand with spokeshaves, but the pattern shown in the photo on the facing page allows me to clean up each leg in a fraction of the time it takes to do it by hand. One-half of the pattern secures the leg for smoothing the front, and the other side is for the back of the leg. And because the pattern ensures uniformity of cuts, duplication is simple.

The leg must not slip or flex throughout the cut. This curved pattern employs individual stops at various points along the curve. This feature compensates for slight variations in the bandsawn surface. Toggle clamps hold the stock down on the pattern, while a stop at one end of the pattern resists the thrust of the cutterhead, preventing the stock from moving laterally (see the drawing on the facing page). Extending the pattern beyond the stock eliminates the need for a starting pin and makes the entry cut smooth and positive.

PATTERN FOR SHAPING BOTH EDGES OF CURVED STOCK

Stop blocks are glued and screwed to base of pattern.

Spindle rotation

Feed direction

Block resists thrust of cutterhead, preventing stock from moving laterally.

¾-in. plywood

Stock

Toggle clamps hold stock to pattern.

Pattern extends beyond workpiece, so starting pin is not necessary.

This pattern cleans up saw marks on curved stock quickly. One-half of the pattern secures the leg for smoothing the front, and the other side is for smoothing the back of the leg.

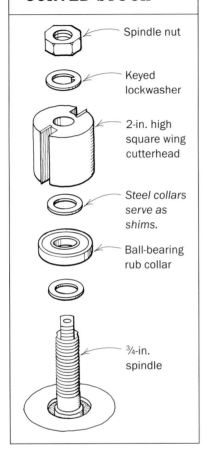

Spindle nut

Keyed
lockwasher

2-in. high
square wing
cutterhead

*Steel collars
serve as
shims.*

Ball-bearing
rub collar

¾-in.
spindle

Safety Checklist for Shaping with a Pattern

• Make sure the pattern is large enough to provide safe placement of your hands.

• Secure the stock firmly on the pattern with stop blocks and toggle clamps.

• Make sure the ring guard is in place.

• Use a starting pin if the pattern does not extend beyond the stock.

• Feed the stock against the spindle rotation.

• Don't make too heavy a cut. If necessary, make the cut in two or more passes.

When setting up the shaper for this cut, I recommend using a 2-in. high square wing cutterhead with Tantung tips. Mount a ball-bearing rub collar of the same diameter underneath the cutterhead and a ring guard above (see the drawing at left). Remember to bandsaw each piece of stock approximately ¹⁄₁₆ in. oversize, which will allow you to make a light shaper cut free of tearout while removing the saw marks.

Shaping with a Fence

The previous methods for shaping curved stock involve referencing the radius edge of the stock or a pattern against a rub collar. However, these methods may not always be practical or even possible. For instance, shaping a wide profile on curved stock against a rub collar would require a dangerously large cutterhead. The photo on the facing page illustrates a curved casing that may be used on a circular window or a series of architectural arches. It would be much safer and more practical to shape this casing from the face with the use of a fence because the knives would be considerably shorter (see the drawing on the facing page). The profiles in the drawing are impossible to shape from the edge, and so they must be shaped from the face.

To shape the curved casing shown on the facing page, begin by selecting clear boards that are wide enough to create a quarter turn

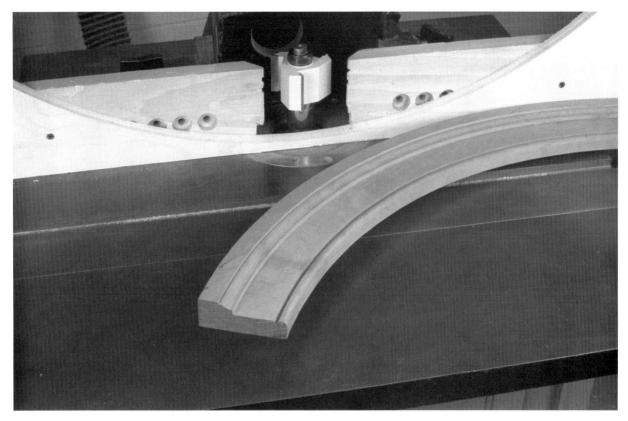

This curved casing is best shaped from the face with the use of a fence.

PROFILES THAT MUST BE SHAPED FROM THE FACE

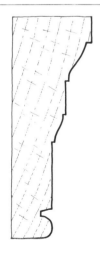

Some profiles are impossible to shape from edge, so they must be shaped from face. Shaping from edge with rub collar would require dangerously long knives.

Window
casing

Quirk with
ogee

Quirk with
bead

When shaping the face of curved stock, maintain contact between the cradle and the stock and use a featherboard. If the stock rises even slightly, the profile will be ruined.

of the circle. By selecting wide lumber, you'll avoid time-consuming and visually distracting joinery in the casing. To lay out the large radius, use a large compass or trammel points that mount on a stick. One of the trammel points will hold a pencil. Set the distance between the points to the outside radius of the casing and scribe an arc directly on the stock. At the same time you set this distance, also mark a length of ¾-in. plywood that will be used as a cradle. Next, set the trammels to the inside radius and mark the stock. Since each of the radii uses the same centerpoint, it's a good idea to clamp the stock to your bench to prevent it from shifting out of position during layout.

The next step is to bandsaw the inside radius of the plywood cradle and the outside radius of the stock. Don't saw the inside radius of the stock until after shaping. Leaving the extra stock at the inside will add mass and give you better hand placement. Then fasten the plywood cradle to the shaper fence with screws. Make

Safety Checklist for Shaping against a Fence

• Make sure the outside radius of the stock matches the radius of the cradle.

• Screw the cradle securely to the shaper fence.

• Check to be sure the cutterhead is securely on the spindle.

• Use a featherboard to hold the stock to the fence.

• Maintain contact between the cradle and the stock.

• Use an extra-long spindle if necessary.

certain that the lowest point of the cradle is centered in the fence opening directly in front of the shaper spindle.

For a curved molding such as this, I find it's best to divide the complex molding into separate basic profiles. This makes the knives much more versatile and enables me to use them for many different applications. For this casing, I'll need cutterheads to shape a ½-in. quirk with bead, a square edge and a ¾-in. ogee.

Begin by shaping the quirk with bead on the inside radius and work outward to maintain support on the fence during each cut. To hold the stock against the fence, clamp a shop-made featherboard on the shaper top (see the photo on the facing page). Because you're shaping on edge, cutting the bead requires mounting the cutterhead high on the spindle, so you'll need to employ steel spacing collars. (If the width of the circular casing exceeds the height of the spindle, use an extra-long spindle.)

When shaping the face of curved stock, it's important to maintain contact between the cradle and the stock, because if the stock accidentally rises—even slightly—the profile will be spoiled. Once the shaping is complete, bandsaw the inside radius of the stock and remove the saw marks with the shaper, using a pattern similar to the one shown on p. 57.

6
Making Moldings

Before the application of moldings, this corner cabinet was just a plain, triangular box.

Moldings play an extremely important role in furniture and architecture. For the custom woodworker, the shaper is the true workhorse for making moldings. Moldings can vary widely in shape and size, from the small thumbnail profile that delicately frames a panel to a series of bold profiles stacked together to create a cornice in a formal room.

In the process of working wood, I'm often fascinated by how moldings can enhance a project. My reproduction of a Virginia corner cabinet is a good example (see the photo at left). Before the moldings were installed, the cabinet was a plain, triangular box. But once the moldings were attached, the plain box was transformed into a formal piece of furniture.

Moldings create tremendous visual interest in several ways. The repeated convex and concave surfaces of moldings can reflect light and create interesting shadowlines (see the top photo on the facing page). The shape, size and placement of moldings can make a piece of furniture appear casual or formal. For example, a simple ogee profile on the edge of a tabletop can eliminate the harsh, utilitarian look of a square edge while still retaining an informal look. Large, complex cornice moldings add dignity to a large case piece. By adding a sticking profile to the bars in a sash door, you effectively reduce the appearance of mass and create a unified look without sacrificing strength. Moldings are also used to provide a transition between elements, such as the upper and lower case of a chest of drawers or the upper and lower sections of a corner cabinet. Regardless of what look you're after, there are a number of ways to both incorporate moldings into your furniture and to create these molding profiles.

Incorporating Moldings into Your Furniture

There are two basic ways to incorporate moldings into your woodworking. The first is to shape the moldings in long strips and attach the strips to the furniture piece (see the photo below). Strip moldings must be mitered to fit and must be secured to the work with glue and/or fasteners (remember to allow for future wood movement). The second method of incorporating moldings into your furniture is to shape the workpiece itself. An example would be the molded edge of a tabletop or the sticking profile on a frame-and-panel door.

Because of its size and power, the shaper is an ideal machine for making moldings, including many large, complex moldings usually produced on an industrial molder. The table saw is an excellent companion to the shaper when making moldings. Excess stock can be removed with the table saw prior to shaping, which makes the

The play of light and shadow created by the molding profiles of this corner cabinet add depth and create visual interest.

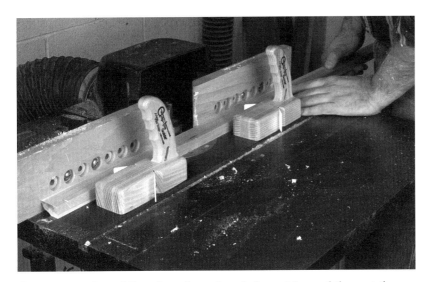

One way to make moldings is to shape them in long strips and then cut the strips to size.

shaping process safer and reduces wear on the shaper tooling and on the machine itself. The table saw can also be used to cut large coves for moldings that might otherwise require a large, expensive cutterhead. Once the cove is created, the shaper can be used to cut additional profiles in the molding.

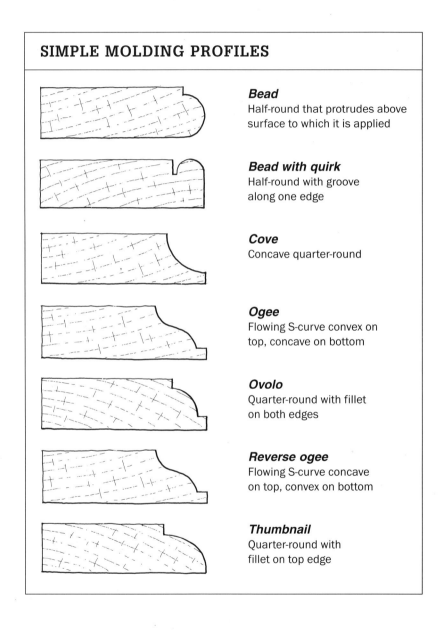

SIMPLE MOLDING PROFILES

Bead
Half-round that protrudes above surface to which it is applied

Bead with quirk
Half-round with groove along one edge

Cove
Concave quarter-round

Ogee
Flowing S-curve convex on top, concave on bottom

Ovolo
Quarter-round with fillet on both edges

Reverse ogee
Flowing S-curve concave on top, convex on bottom

Thumbnail
Quarter-round with fillet on top edge

Creating Molding Profiles

There are two types of molding profiles: simple and complex. The simple profiles are uncomplicated shapes and forms (see the drawing on the facing page). Complex moldings are simply combinations of the simple profiles shown in the drawing. Complex moldings can be relatively easy to produce with basic cutterheads by dividing the complicated profile into smaller, simpler profiles. This method is also safer and easier on your woodworking budget than shaping with larger, more expensive cutterheads that are dedicated to producing a single profile. By stocking several sizes of each simple profile (½-in. to 2-in. ogee, for example), you can reproduce almost any complex molding that you may encounter in your work.

Creating complex profiles in this manner requires that you plan the cutting direction and sequence of each cut. Some profiles such as the ogee may be cut from the face or the edge. However, other profiles such as the bead must be shaped from the face. It's also very important to have sufficient flat surfaces to contact the shaper fence and table during each cut. Failing to do so risks having the stock tilt during the cut and spoiling the molding or causing an accident.

SEPARATE THE PROFILES

If the molding is extremely complicated, I find it helpful to draw sketches to plan a safe cutting sequence (see the drawing on p. 66).

As you draw your profile, look for ways to separate a complex profile into simple profiles. The molding in the example in the drawing consists of two coves, two beads and an ovolo, with fillets between the individual profiles as transitions. I started with a rectangular plank measuring 1¾ in. by 4 in. by 4 ft., which is the finished molding dimensions plus enough length to miter around the cabinet (this is a strip molding).

CUTTING SEQUENCE

The trick or challenge to producing complex moldings with the shaper is to sequence the cuts in an order that always allows sufficient stock to rest on the table and fence. With few exceptions, the heaviest profiles should be shaped first. When making a molding profile, it's best to make the heaviest cut first so that the stock will have plenty of mass to resist chatter and kickback. You may also consider making each cut in two passes, especially if the profile is somewhat deep. In this case the cove and bead should be shaped first.

SHAPING A COMPLEX MOLDING

On complex moldings, each profile is shaped separately. Sequence is shown here.

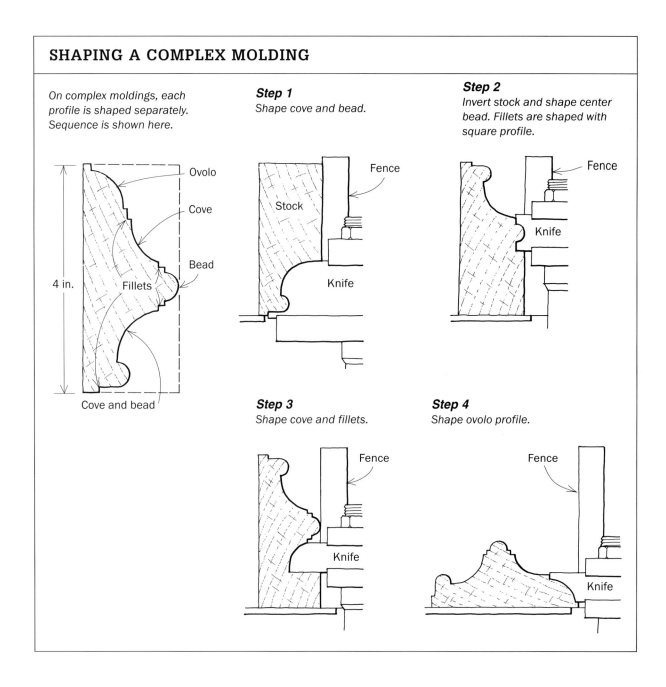

Step 1
Shape cove and bead.

Step 2
Invert stock and shape center bead. Fillets are shaped with square profile.

Step 3
Shape cove and fillets.

Step 4
Shape ovolo profile.

Next, invert the molding and shape the small center bead. Inverting the stock places the flat, unshaped portion against the shaper table and fence, which provides stability.

With the center bead shaped, mount a square cutterhead and make the fillets that flank it. Then cut the cove profile with a cove cutter. Although the cove profile could be shaped from either the face or the edge, approaching from the edge would require very long shaper knives, which could be dangerous.

ARCHITECTURAL CORNICE

This cornice can be made on shaper from six separate molding strips using simple knife profiles. Dentil can be made on table saw with dado head.

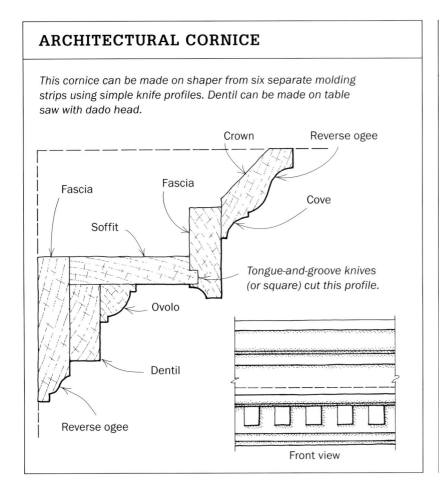

Crown

Reverse ogee

Fascia

Fascia

Cove

Soffit

Tongue-and-groove knives (or square) cut this profile.

Ovolo

Dentil

Reverse ogee

Front view

CORNICE MOLDING

This cornice profile is easy to make and much less wasteful when shaped in two separate molding strips.

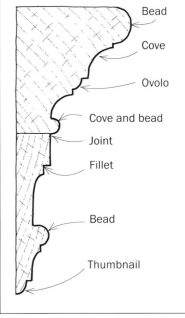

Bead

Cove

Ovolo

Cove and bead

Joint

Fillet

Bead

Thumbnail

To shape the ovolo profile and the fillets on the top edge, position the back of the molding flat on the table. The result is a crisp, distinctive, 18th-century molding that is authentic in detail and in proportion to the original.

Another method of making large, complex moldings is to make each basic profile on a separate strip and stack the strips together. The architectural cornice molding shown in the left drawing above can be made this way. A key point to remember when using this method is to match the color of the stock carefully if it is not going to be painted. Otherwise, the molding may appear disjointed.

Another interesting cornice profile is that on the corner cabinet shown on p. 62. To make the cornice profile, I combined two separate molding strips, which results in an authentic cornice that provides the crowning touch of formality to this piece (see the right drawing above).

7

Grinding Custom Knives

A tooling manufacturer custom-made this cope cutterhead.

The knives for this lockedge cutterhead were custom-ground.

Once you have gained experience with the shaper, you'll most likely begin to feel limited by the relatively small selection of commercially available cutterhead profiles. This is especially true if you design your own furniture or if you need to match old profiles on period furniture or architecture.

One viable alternative, especially for a profile that you'll use often, is to have the cutterhead custom-made (see the top photo at left). Most shaper tooling manufacturers offer this service, and although it isn't inexpensive, the price may be well worth it for the uniqueness and value that the profile adds to your work.

A less-expensive alternative is to use a system of locking collars and high-speed steel (HSS) knives and grind the profile yourself. Called a lockedge cutterhead, the system works like this: A pair of knives is secured between two disks, called collars. Serrations on the knives engage with a worm screw in one of the collars, and the collars are held together with machine screws (see the bottom photo at left). The complete cutterhead—knives, collars and screws—is placed on the shaper spindle and locked in place with the spindle nut. Learning to use the system is not difficult, and it gives you enormous shaping flexibility in addition to adding a whole new dimension to your woodworking.

I build mostly period reproductions, and many profiles found on antique furniture are just not available in stock cutterheads, so I use this cutterhead system frequently. Recently I milled the trim for the

This window casing was milled with custom-ground knives. Grinding custom profiles enables you to shape unique or old casing profiles at a fraction of the cost of having the molding custom-milled.

interior of my house with knives that I ground myself, which enabled me to shape unique, old casing profiles at a fraction of the cost of having them custom-milled (see the photo above).

There are other advantages to lockedge cutterheads. You can order a ball-bearing collar (called a rub collar) that is an integral part of the cutterhead, so you no longer have to buy a separate rub collar for each profile, as is the case with wing cutterheads. Additionally, with a maximum pattern depth of 1½ in. and a maximum knife width of 3½ in., there is seldom a profile that I can't match. As I mentioned before, this system is a fraction of the cost of wing cutterheads, so I'm able to afford more profiles than I could with wing cutterheads. Finally, using this system is good for business. I operate a small, custom shop, and people come to me with shaping jobs they can't have done anywhere else locally.

However, despite the advantages, it's important that you understand that there are safety risks associated with lockedge cutterheads, and this system should only be tried after you've gained plenty of shaper experience with wing cutterheads. But I believe that the use of lockedge cutterheads can be a safe, productive aspect of woodworking. Before you can begin grinding knives for lockedge cutterheads, you must know about cutting theory and the tools needed for the job. But it's also important to know about the parts involved in the cutterhead system. Let's begin with the collars, then I'll talk about the knives.

Selecting Collars

Collars are available in both lockedge and smooth edge. The lockedge is a big improvement over the old, smooth-edge system because the serrations on the knives lock with a worm screw in one of the collars to prevent the knives from flying out. I highly recommend the lockedge system for its maximum holding ability. As a matter of fact, I use this system more than any other cutterhead setup because of the economy and flexibility it provides. After nearly 20 years, I've never experienced even a minor accident. However, I'm *always* strict in following the manufacturer's safety guidelines.

Collars for lockedge knives are manufactured in many sizes, but you'll probably only need one or two; getting the most flexibility means making the best selection. Collar diameters range from 2 in. to 4 in. and are graduated in ½-in. increments (see the photo below). For a ¾-in. spindle shaper, a 2½-in. diameter collar works well. The large 4-in. collars are designed for shaping wide profiles on industrial shapers with 1¼-in. spindles. I strongly discourage shaping wide profiles until you've gained substantial experience with this system. If you plan to shape curved work, make sure to specify a rub collar. Under no circumstance should you use bushings on collars; always buy the bore to fit the spindle of your shaper.

A 2½-in. collar (left) is good for straight work, but the 2-in. rub collar (right) is best if you have to shape curves.

When ordering collars for the lockedge system, you will have to specify rotation. I usually buy collars for counterclockwise rotation because I typically feed stock from right to left. Besides, if I need to run clockwise, I simply invert the collar on the spindle. It's important to note, however, that rub collars are manufactured with the ball bearing on the bottom. If you want the bearing on top with a counterclockwise rotation, you'll have to specify a clockwise rotation and then invert the collar on the spindle. *Always* run lockedge collars in the direction of the arrow stamped on the collar.

Selecting Knife Stock

Knives for lockedge cutterheads must always be used in pairs of the same weight, profile and dimension. The type of knives you use will depend on which style cutterhead you have: lockedge or smooth edge. But that doesn't mean there aren't any variables. You'll need to decide on the thickness, width and length of the bar stock to grind. The important thing to keep in mind here is that the knives must be a matched pair. Never use knife stock of different thickness, width or length in the same collar. To ensure proper balance, the knives should be of the same weight.

HSS knife stock is available in thicknesses of ¼ in., ⁵⁄₁₆ in. and ⅜ in., and that thickness determines the maximum distance that the knives can safely project from the collars. The knives should project from the collars no more than three to four times the knife thickness. That means that the ⅜-in. thick knife stock can be used to create profiles that are 50% deeper than that of the ¼-in. stock. That being the case, you may think it's wise to buy the thicker stock and have the flexibility to grind a deep profile when the need arises. However, the cost of the ⅜-in. stock is approximately twice as much, and it takes more time to grind the thicker steel. If your work doesn't require the ⅜-in. thick knife stock, save yourself some time and money by purchasing the thinner stock—either ¼ in. or ⁵⁄₁₆ in.

A pair of knives should be cut from the same bar stock to ensure that they are the same width (in thousands of an inch) so that they will be equally secured in the collars. The width of HSS knife stock ranges from ½ in. to 3½ in. in ½-in. increments. Because of its small size, the ½-in. wide stock isn't available in lockedge. It's available only in smooth edge, so you will need to purchase a smooth-edge collar if you intend to use stock of this width. In general, I've found that it is often better to use lockedge stock that is slightly wider than the profile to be ground (see the drawing at right). There are two reasons for this. First, the serrations on one edge of the stock do not allow the full width of the knife to be used

Don't grind knife profile full width of stock, like this point. Sharp point could overheat during use or break off.

Instead, use large knife stock and leave sufficient support for full height of knife.

in the profile. Second, you should avoid grinding sharp, pointed projections on the edge of a knife. A sharp projection will be prone to overheating during use and could burn the workpiece. Even worse, it could break off while you're shaping.

HSS knife stock is sold in 25-in. lengths, so it must be cut prior to use. For an additional charge, you may request that the manufacturer cut the steel to length if you're sure of the sizes you will need. I usually buy several bars of steel of various widths and cut it into shorter lengths myself as I need it. I use an abrasive cutoff wheel for this purpose.

Cutting Theory

Before you can grind custom profiles on knives, you'll need to know the basic cutting theory and how cutting affects the knife profile. Knives mount in the collars to create a cutting angle of 30°. The angle is formed by a radial line drawn from the center of the collars to the face of the knives (see the top left drawing on the facing page). Because each knife is mounted at a 30° angle, the knife profile must be deeper than the molding profile to be shaped (see the top right drawing on the facing page). Simply put, the amount that the knives project from the collars must be greater than the width of the profile to be shaped. This is important because it helps determine the knife length.

Also, to achieve a smooth surface on the molding profile to be shaped, the knives must be ground slightly with two bevels: one is the grind bevel, and the other is the relief bevel.

GRIND BEVEL

As the cutterhead rotates, the heel of each knife must clear the workpiece. Otherwise, the knife will pound the stock with each revolution and burnish the stock, or worse, burn it. Whether you're grinding a bench chisel or a lockedge knife, the goal is to produce a sturdy, sharp edge that resists chipping. To achieve this goal, the knife profile must have the proper grind bevel—the angle formed by the bevel and the knife face (see the bottom drawing on the facing page).

If you've sharpened hand tools, you're already familiar with this concept. A shallow bevel shears the wood cleanly, but if it's too shallow, the knife edge will wear quickly. A knife edge will last

CUTTING GEOMETRY OF LOCKEDGE COLLARS

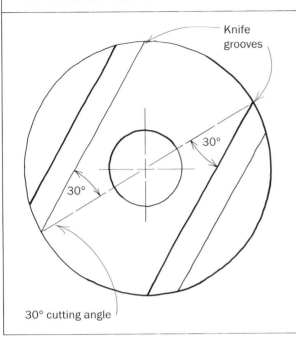

Knife grooves

30°

30°

30° cutting angle

SETTING THE KNIFE DEPTH

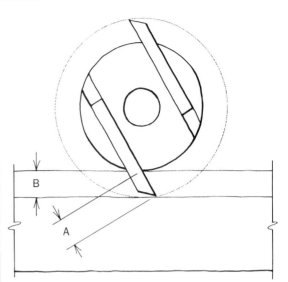

B

A

Knife projection from collars must be greater than width of profile to be shaped. Knife depth (A) is deeper than molding profile (B).

GRIND BEVEL

Grind bevel of 30° provides clearance so that heel of knife does not burn or burnish the stock from continuous contact.

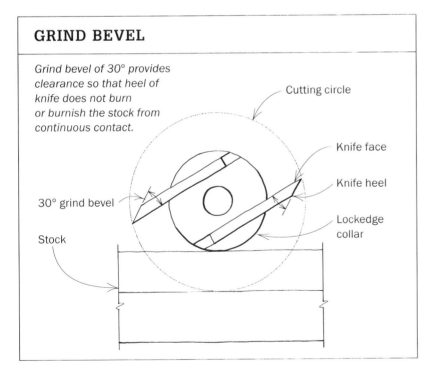

Cutting circle

Knife face

Knife heel

Lockedge collar

30° grind bevel

Stock

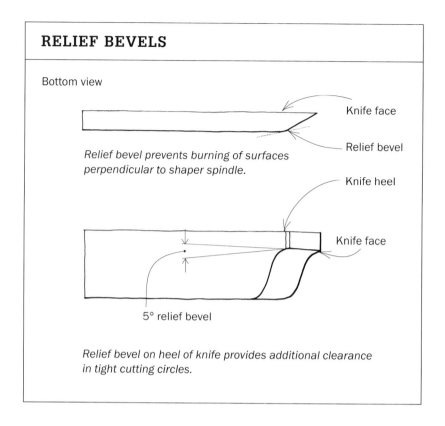

RELIEF BEVELS

Bottom view

Knife face

Relief bevel

Relief bevel prevents burning of surfaces perpendicular to shaper spindle.

Knife heel

Knife face

5° relief bevel

Relief bevel on heel of knife provides additional clearance in tight cutting circles.

longer with a steep, blunt bevel but doesn't cut as cleanly, and the heel of the bevel may burnish the stock. I've found that a 30° grind bevel usually creates sufficient clearance and is a good compromise between a sharp cut and a durable edge.

RELIEF BEVEL

There are times (such as when you've got a tight cutting circle) when you'll need additional clearance at the heel of the knife so that the heel will clear the stock without burnishing it. In these cases, grind away a bit more from the heel to create a secondary, or relief, bevel. A relief bevel of approximately 5° should be sufficient to prevent the heel of the knife from burning or burnishing the stock. A relief bevel is also necessary on cutting surfaces that are perpendicular to the shaper spindle (see the drawing above).

Finding the Knife Profile

With a solid grasp of cutting theory, you can turn your attention to finding the knife profile. I do a lot of custom reproduction work and often have to match old moldings. I use a couple of methods to create a knife profile that matches the molding profile. One fast, simple method I use when I have a sample molding I want to reproduce is to cut the end of the sample at 30° (see the drawing at right), which will reveal the true knife profile. If you don't have a molding sample available that you can cut, you can draw the molding profile full size and project the knife profile from this drawing.

DRAW KNIFE PROFILE

Begin by drawing bisecting horizontal and vertical lines (lines A and B in the drawings on p. 76) perpendicular to one another. Next, draw the molding profile in the upper left quadrant. In the lower left quadrant, draw a line from the centerpoint that forms a 30° angle with the horizontal line (B). Then divide the molding profile into vertical segments and project these lines to the 30° line. From the centerpoint, use a compass to swing each division line to the right-hand side of the drawing. Next, divide the molding profile into horizontal segments and extend these lines to the upper right quadrant. From the intersection points of the projection line, draw vertical lines through the horizontal lines extended from the molding profile. Connect the intersection points to create the outline of the knife profile. For pinpoint accuracy, I keep my pencil sharp and divide the drawing of the molding into small segments.

DETERMINE KNIFE LENGTH

After drawing the knife profile, the next step is to determine the total knife length. This is actually pretty simple. First measure the collar groove, then add the profile depth to that. Remember that the knife profile will be longer than the molding profile (see the top right drawing on p. 73). Cut two pieces of knife stock to this length; I normally use an abrasive cutoff wheel for this.

Before sketching the profile on the knife edge, determine how the knives will be oriented in the collars. I'm used to feeding the stock from right to left with a counterclockwise spindle rotation, so I grind the knives accordingly. I coat the knife face with machinist's layout dye and scratch the profile into the dye with an awl.

Remember, knives must extend at least halfway into the collars for safety. I make new knives to fill the entire length of the groove. But through repeated sharpening, the knives will become shortened

MATCHING KNIFE PROFILE TO SAMPLE MOLDING

Cut section of molding at 30° angle and use it as template for grinding knife profile.

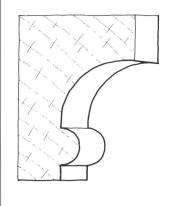

Step 1

Draw two intersecting, perpendicular lines (A and B).

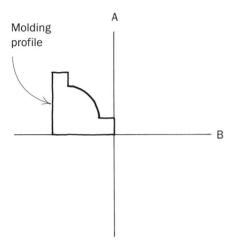

Step 2

Draw a line in the lower left quadrant 30° from horizontal line (B).

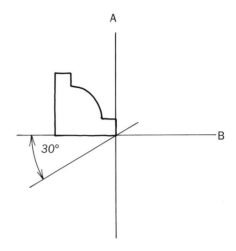

Step 3

Divide molding into vertical segments and project to 30° line. Use compass to swing each line to right side.

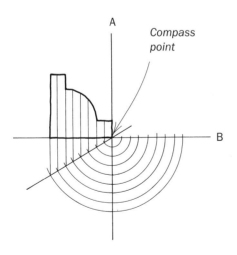

Step 4

Divide molding profile into horizontal segments. Extend projection lines to horizontal lines from molding profile and connect intersection points to create knife profile.

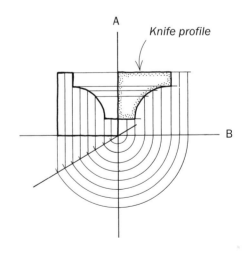

and will no longer fill half the collar groove (for most readers this might take several years). At that point discard them. Using short knives risks having them thrown from the collars at a high velocity.

Once the knife stock is cut to length and the profile is laid out, you can begin grinding. Let's take a look at the tools involved.

Grinding Tools

The tools needed for grinding lockedge knives are minimal. You will need a stationary bench grinder—a 6-in. or 8-in. grinder will do. More important than the grinder itself is the type of wheel you fit it with. The cheap, gray wheels that are standard on most grinders cut too slow, need frequent cleaning and shaping (a process called dressing) and tend to overheat the steel. Even though they are expensive, I prefer the pink or white aluminum-oxide wheels because they cut fast and have less tendency to become clogged during use.

I use a ¾-in. wide wheel on one end of the grinder and a ¼-in. wheel on the other. To allow grinding of fluid curves found on traditional molding profiles, I round the corners of the wheels with a dressing stick. To grind small details in the knife stock, an abrasive cutoff wheel may be used.

To achieve the best surface on the wood during shaping, the knives must be honed after grinding. For honing, use slipstones, which are available in a variety of natural and man-made materials; I prefer fast-cutting ceramic stones. Finally, for the cutterhead to be balanced, the knives must weigh the same, so you'll need a small, inexpensive scale.

Begin grinding by roughing out the knife profile. Don't worry about the grind bevel until you reach the layout line.

Grinding a Knife

In my classes and seminars, people always ask how I grind two knives alike. It's a valid question, and I always tell people that it isn't as difficult as it first appears. Let me first point out that it is not necessary (or possible) to grind the profiles to tolerances used in the metalworking trade. Instead, each knife must be carefully ground to match the drawing or molding sample as close as humanly possible. If the knives follow the outline of the drawing or molding sample, you'll end up with a finished molding that you'll be satisfied with.

Before you begin grinding, here are some safety reminders. First, wear a face shield. Before turning on the grinder, step to one side. This will allow any debris from a broken wheel to fly past you,

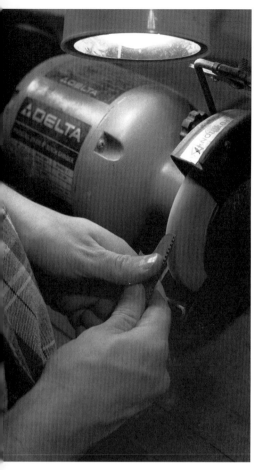

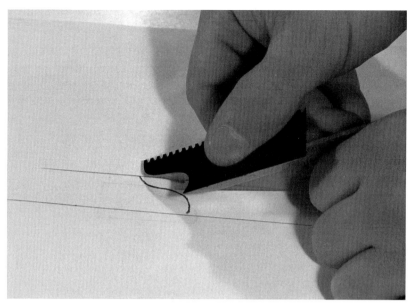

To check the knife profile, hold the knife over the molding drawing, supported by a 30° draftsman's triangle. By sighting directly over the knife, you'll see where you need to grind away more steel.

As you near the layout line, begin to create the grind bevel by holding the knife stock at a 30° angle.

not at you, when you start the grinder. If a wheel is cracked, it will usually break upon, or soon after, startup. (I've never had one break.) Also, be sure your grinder is fitted with the necessary guards and make sure you've got sufficient lighting. The two major steps to grinding a profile are roughing out and honing.

ROUGH OUT THE PROFILE

To rough out the profile, hold the knife edge toward the center of the grinding wheel (see the photo on p. 77). Concentrate on creating the profile. Don't worry about the grind bevel until you begin to reach the layout line on the stock.

As you close in on the layout line, hold the knife stock at an angle to create the 30° grind bevel (see the left photo above). Experience tells me how to hold the knife to achieve the grind bevel, but I always check it about halfway through.

It's easy to check the knife profile with a 30° draftsman's triangle. Simply hold the knife over the molding drawing, supporting the knife with the triangle (see the right photo above). By sighting directly over the knife, you'll see exactly where you need to grind away more steel. This method is fast and surprisingly accurate. I normally go back to the grinder once or twice to touch up the knife so that it matches the drawing exactly.

Finally, carefully grind relief bevels into any surfaces that are perpendicular to the spindle and on the heel of the knife edge, if necessary. To grind the relief bevels, touch the knife bevel to the grinding wheel and pivot it sideways just slightly. Next, weigh the knives carefully, and if necessary, grind away the blank end of the heavier knife to bring it to the same weight as the lighter knife to balance the pair.

Keep a container of water next to the grinder to cool the steel as it begins to get hot. I grind the knife profile freehand, using both hands for control. If you prefer, you can use a tool rest or a grinding jig. When the steel blank gets almost too hot to hold, it is time for quenching. I find it's best to work back and forth between the two knives, quenching one while I grind the other.

HONE THE EDGES

The last step is to hone the knives and remove the rough edge left from grinding (called a burr). A small assortment of three or four honing stones of various shapes will allow you to touch up most any profile. I prefer ceramic stones because they are resistant to wear, yet they cut fast. Remember to hone the back of the knife as well as the bevel, just as when sharpening a bench chisel or a carving tool. Finally, rinse the knives and wipe them dry.

Place the knives in the bottom collar first. A knife must extend at least halfway into the collars for safe shaping.

To make sure the knives project from the collars exactly the same distance use a dial indicator, which measures thousands of an inch.

Mounting the Knives in the Collars

Mounting the knives in the collars correctly is critical for safe use of the lockedge system. The knives and the collar grooves must be clean. Check them for dust, pitch, oil or any other foreign material that may cause the knives to slip. Also check for small burrs on collar grooves that could prevent the knives from seating firmly. If you find any, grind them away or discard the collars.

First place the knives in the bottom collar and position them in their approximate locations in the collar grooves (see the photo on p. 79). Then place the top collar in position so that the grooves align with the knives. Screw in the retaining bolts and leave them slightly loose, then put the assembly on the spindle.

The knives should extend an equal distance from the collars for proper balancing. A well-balanced lockedge cutterhead is safe, smooth running and reduces spindle-bearing wear. A dial indicator is a good tool for this critical stage of the setup. It is a device that measures in thousands of an inch (0.001 in.). Place the dial indicator on the shaper table, with the plunger tip on the end of one of the knives (see the photo above). Make minor adjustments to the positions of the knives so that their cutting edges extend just enough to create the profile. The worm screw on lockedge collars makes it easy to adjust the knives. Set the dial indicator face to zero

Safety List for Shaping with Lockedge Cutterheads

- Knives must always be used in pairs of the same weight, profile and dimension. Knife pairs must be cut from the same bar stock.

- Each knife must extend at least halfway into the collar groove. Using short knives risks having a knife thrown from the collar.

- Knives should extend beyond the collar no more than three to four times the knife thickness.

- Each knife should extend an equal distance from the collar for balance.

- When shaping with lockedge cutterheads, the spindle speed should not exceed 6,000 rpm.

- Make sure that the collar grooves are free of any foreign matter that may cause slippage of the knives. Also, check the collar grooves for burrs or wear and grind the burrs away, if necessary, or replace the collars.

- Until you gain plenty of experience, limit yourself to small knives (2 in. wide or less).

and rotate the cutterhead on the spindle 180° to check the second knife. If the knives don't align, make the necessary adjustments. If you don't have a dial indicator, clamp a stick to the shaper top so that it touches the end of one knife. Spin the cutterhead by hand and check the second knife. This method works fine for smaller knives (1 in. or less in width), but as the knife size increases, balance becomes more critical.

After you've ensured that the second knife is positioned in its groove equal to the first knife, tighten the retaining bolts, working back and forth to tighten them gradually. This ensures that the collars grip the knives equally and that the collars stay in alignment with each other. (Be careful not to cut yourself on the knives.)

You really can only snug the bolts down so much while the cutterhead assembly is on the spindle. To tighten the bolts further, place the assembly in a vise with wood-protected faces and firmly snug them down. It's okay to use a long Allen wrench for this, but don't extend the wrench with a pipe or other means. Increasing your leverage by extending the wrench with a pipe can stretch the bolts beyond their elastic limit. This distortion can create metal fatigue, possibly causing the bolts to snap while you are shaping.

8

Frame-and-Panel Joinery

This is a typical frame-and-panel door with coped sticking.

No book on the shaper would be complete without a chapter on frame-and-panel joinery. And the shaper, with its enormous power, is the best machine for producing the decorative molded edge on the frame as well as the beveled edges of the panel.

The frame-and-panel design has been around for centuries. It's seen in doors for both furniture and architecture (see the photo at left), casework (the rolltop desk is made almost entirely of a series of panels surrounded by framework) and wall paneling. Because the frame-and-panel look is so popular, even modern architectural components, such as steel entry doors, are stamped into this configuration.

The enduring popularity of the frame-and-panel design is easy to understand: It allows for seasonal wood movement in a large expanse while adding a look of formality and distinction. The panel is the centerpiece, and the frame consists of stiles and rails. The stiles run top to bottom, and the rails run horizontally between the stiles (see the drawing on the facing page). A mullion is a vertical frame member used to break up a large panel. If mortise-and-tenon joinery is to be used in the frame-and-panel, mortises are cut in the stiles, and the tenons are cut on the rails. In a frame-and-panel with mullions, the rails are mortised to receive the tenons on the mullion ends.

FRAME-AND-PANEL CONFIGURATION

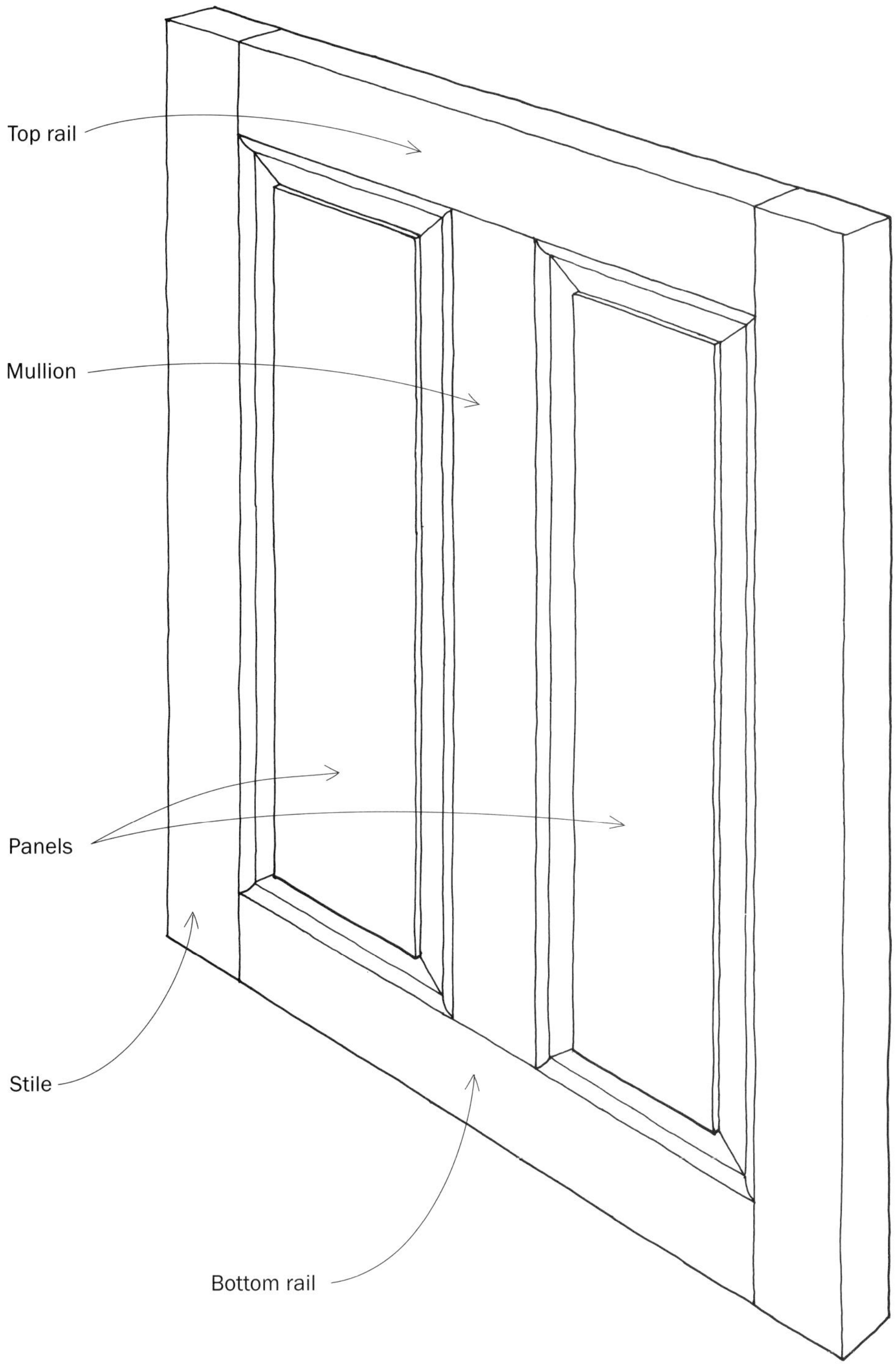

Top rail

Mullion

Panels

Stile

Bottom rail

In this chapter, you'll learn how to use the shaper to create cope-and-stick frames and a variety of raised panels. But before I get into the details of constructing the frame-and-panel, I'll briefly discuss how to proportion panels to ensure aesthetic success.

Proportioning Frame-and-Panels

Frame-and-panels look best if they are rectangular in form rather than square. For example, a large square opening in the base of a corner cabinet would be more visually appealing if it were fitted with two rectangular doors or one door with two rectangular panels separated by a mullion (see the drawing on p. 83). Perhaps the most visually pleasing rectangle is that based on the golden mean, which is a ratio (1:1.618) used by the ancient Greeks to achieve visual harmony in their temples and public buildings. The golden mean is still used today by architects and designers (even credit cards are designed around the golden mean).

The golden mean can be used to create a golden rectangle, which in turn can help you create a perfectly proportioned panel.

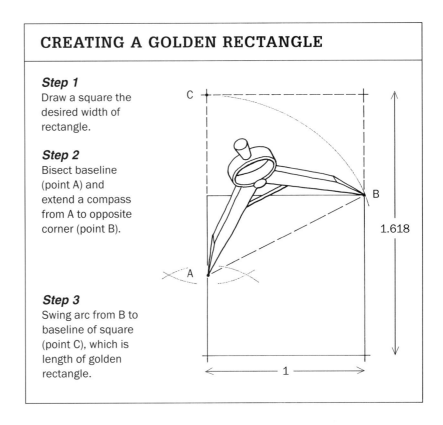

CREATING A GOLDEN RECTANGLE

Step 1
Draw a square the desired width of rectangle.

Step 2
Bisect baseline (point A) and extend a compass from A to opposite corner (point B).

Step 3
Swing arc from B to baseline of square (point C), which is length of golden rectangle.

In a golden rectangle, the ratio of width to length is 1:1.618. If you know the width, you can find the height of a panel by multiplying the width by 1.618. You may also work from a known height and divide it by 1.618 to find the width. Another option is to draw a square, with sides equal to the width of your panel. Bisect one side of the square (the baseline) and extend a compass from that point to an opposite corner. Then swing an arc with the compass from the corner to the baseline of the square, which will give you the length of the golden rectangle (see the drawing on the facing page).

As useful as the golden mean is, it can be overused, or it may not work effectively within your required dimensions. Another proportioning method that can be used is ratios of whole numbers, such as 1:2, 2:3, 3:4, 5:8. These ratios will also be of help in creating well-proportioned frame-and-panels.

With the proportions worked out, it's time to consider the joinery you'll use. I have found that cope-and-stick joinery works best for frame-and-panel construction.

Making a Frame with Cope-and-Stick Joinery

As I mentioned earlier, the shaper is the ideal tool for making frame-and-panels. That's because its combination of raw power and stacking cutterheads allows you to efficiently and safely cut cope-and-stick joinery—my first choice whenever I'm making a large number of frame-and-panel doors or similar architectural work.

Sticking is a decorative profile on the inside edges of all the frame pieces. It softens the edges of the frame, offers a nice embellishment and creates a groove to accept the panel that's added later. The coping is a reverse profile cut on the ends of the rails to match the sticking on the stiles (see the drawing on p. 87). One advantage of this profile/reverse-profile cut is that it gives the appearance of a clean miter in the corners of the frame (see the photo on p. 82).

Although the ovolo, ogee, reverse ogee and thumbnail profiles are most commonly used for sticking, the profile can be as simple as a chamfer (see the drawing at right). Regardless of which profile you choose, it should always be proportioned to fit well within the dimensions of the frame. For the average piece of furniture, the sticking profiles are usually ¼ in., 5⁄16 in. or ⅜ in.

There are two basic ways to cut cope-and-stick joinery on the shaper. One way is to use two sets of stacked cutterheads. One set of cutterheads shapes the sticking and the panel groove; the other set shapes the coping and a stub tenon on the ends of rails and

COMMON STICKING PROFILES

Ovolo

Ogee

Reverse ogee

Thumbnail

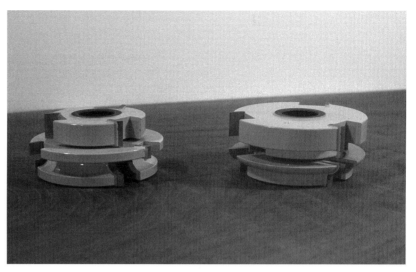

Coping and sticking with matching stacked cutterheads is fast and efficient. The set on the left cuts the sticking and the panel groove. The set on the right cuts the coping and the stub tenon.

The stub tenon (right) on the rails or mullion is usually no longer than the depth of the panel groove. A typical tenon (left) is much longer.

mullions (see the right photo above). The stub tenon is no longer than the depth of the panel groove, usually ⁵⁄₁₆ in. (see the left photo above). Using stacked cutterheads for both the coping and the sticking is fast and efficient and allows you to make a surprisingly strong joint because of the precise fit created by the matching cutterheads.

To increase the strength of this joint further, many woodworkers substitute a plywood panel for the traditional solid panel. This allows them to glue the panel in the frame grooves. Since there's no problem with wood movement in plywood, you can glue the panel in place to create a sturdy frame-and-panel assembly.

Although cope-and-stick joinery with stub tenons works well for small frame-and-panel work, I prefer the mechanical strength that the traditional mortise-and-tenon joint offers for my larger projects. Integrating the mortise and tenon into the cope-and-stick joint is straightforward. The sticking is cut just as you would for a standard cope-and-stick joint. The difference is how the coping is cut.

To allow for the longer tenon (this is cut on the table saw), you'll need to use a special coping cutterhead and a stub spindle (for more on this method, see pp. 88-89). The following are the steps I take to make a frame with traditional cope-and-stick joinery.

LAY OUT AND CUT FRAME STOCK TO PROPER DIMENSION
Before shaping, lay out and cut your frame stock. Begin with the stiles. Lay out the total height of the assembly and cut the stiles to

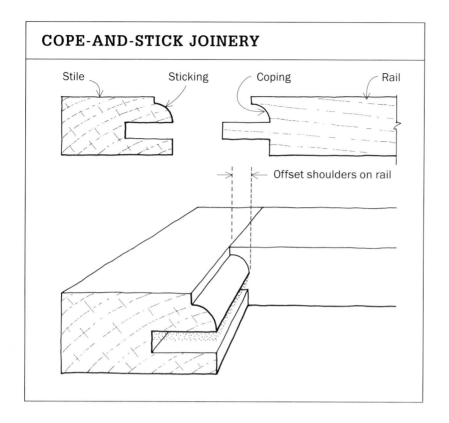

COPE-AND-STICK JOINERY

Stile　　　　Sticking　　　　Coping　　　　Rail

Offset shoulders on rail

length. Then measure and mark the location of the rails (and mullions, if any). To figure the rail length, double the stile width and subtract that from the door width. Add to that number the length of each tenon on the ends of the rail (the shoulder on the tenon is offset to compensate for the sticking width, as shown in the drawing above). When cutting the frame stock, use stops to ensure uniformity.

Although ¾ in. is a standard frame thickness, I normally use ⅞-in. stock (planed to dimension) because I like the substantial feel this offers, and the added thickness will resist warping better than ¾-in. stock. (Since most stacked sets of cutterheads will accept stock up to 1 in. thick, using heavier stock isn't a problem.)

SHAPE THE COPING

With all frame pieces cut to length, it's time to begin shaping. I find it's best to shape the coping before the sticking. This way any tearout at the end grain from coping is removed with the edge-shaping from the sticking. As I've said previously, end grain is tough and will burn easily. So it's important to make sure the coping cutterheads are very sharp.

Using a Stub Spindle and Coping Cutterhead

The strength and structural integrity of traditional mortise-and-tenon joinery is well-known. And when strength and durability are especially important in a piece—and when I've got a bit more time—I typically cut the long tenon on the table saw and use a stub spindle on the shaper in conjunction with a special coping cutterhead to shape the coping (see the photo at right). Constructing a frame-and-panel door in this manner is a bit more complicated, but I feel it's worth the extra effort for fine work.

To use this technique, you must have a stub spindle for your shaper. This inexpensive accessory temporarily replaces the standard spindle in your machine. The stub spindle is threaded internally, and the coping cutterhead is secured to the spindle with a cap screw. The coping cutterhead winds up flush to the end of the stub spindle. This unique system allows a tenon to pass over the cutterhead unobstructed by the shaper spindle (see the bottom photo on the facing page).

A long tenon on the coping allows for a stronger joint in the frame assembly.

To cope the rails and mullions using this setup, first mount the stub spindle and coping cutterhead in the shaper. Use a miter gauge to guide the stock and a fence to control the cutting depth. The fence I use is simply a piece of ¼-in. plywood with a very small opening for the spindle and cutterhead (see the top photo on the facing page). This simple fence provides support for narrow frame stock while allowing long tenons to pass over the cutterhead. For accuracy, the fence must be adjusted parallel to the miter-gauge slot. Make final adjustments to the fence and spindle, raising the cutterhead so that it just touches the bottom of the tenon. Once you're confident with the setup, make a cut on a test piece and check it against the sticking template (for future setups, it's a good idea to make a sticking template).

A ¼-in. plywood fence supports narrow frame stock while allowing long tenons to pass over the cutterhead.

When making the cuts, attach a wood backup board to the miter gauge. The backup board will help support the stock and prevent tearout on the trailing edge of the cut (see the photo at right). Position the end of the backup board as close as possible to the shaper fence. Then shape the coping on the rails (mullions too, if any).

Attach a backup board to the miter gauge to prevent tearout on the trailing edge of the coping.

Cope rails and mullions using a jig to eliminate tearout at the trailing end and to make the operation safer. The jig slides in the miter-gauge slot.

To eliminate tearout at the trailing end of the coping and to make the operation safer, I cope the rails and the mullions using a sliding jig. This jig is easy to make and holds the stock securely. It consists of a plywood base and a cleat. Toggle clamps hold the stock against the cleat, and the whole setup slides in the miter-gauge slot on the shaper table (see the photo above). The jig is used in conjunction with the shaper fence, which works as a depth stop and adds a measure of safety by surrounding the cutterhead and directing the shavings to the dust collector.

Begin by stacking the set of coping cutterheads on the shaper spindle. This set consists of two square cutters to cut the tenon and the shoulder, and a coping cutter. The coping cutter goes on the spindle first, followed by the small-diameter square cutter and then the large-diameter square cutter. Tighten the locknut and adjust the spindle height by lining up the cutters with a sticking profile template. If you don't have a sticking template, you should position the cut on the stock so that the panel is flush with the face of the frame stock. For instance, say you're using a ⅝-in. thick panel. To bring the panel flush with the face of the ⅞-in. frame, offset the mortise and the panel groove from the back of the frame by ¼ in.

When sticking narrow frame members, use push blocks or a power feeder to keep your hands away from the cutterhead.

Also, reduce the width of the tenon by the depth of the panel groove. (I recommend making a sticking profile template for each stacked cutterhead set so that you'll be able to match the coping to it without having to set up the shaper for a sticking cut first.) Remember that the stock will be elevated by the sliding jig, so adjust the spindle height accordingly. Now lock the spindle height and set the fence into position for use as a stop. Then secure the fence and make a test cut to match the sticking template. You'll most likely have to make minor adjustments to the fence and/or spindle height. Once you're satisfied with the setup, cut the coping on all the rails and mullions.

SHAPE THE STICKING

To shape the sticking, first stack the sticking cutterhead set according to the manufacturer's instructions. One cutter shapes the sticking profile, a second cutter plows the groove for the panel, and a third planes the square shoulder below the groove. I prefer to shape the stock facedown so that any minor variations in stock thickness wind up hidden on the back of the frame.

With the stacked cutterhead in position, tighten the spindle nut and position the split fence to expose the cutterhead at the smallest cutting circle. I shape just enough of a test piece to reach the outfeed fence, turn off the shaper and adjust the outfeed fence forward until it touches the test piece. Then I lock the fence in position. If you have sticking template available, you can use it as a guide for making the fence and spindle-height adjustments. Also, when shaping the narrow frame members, use push blocks or a power feeder to keep your hands a safe distance from the cutterhead (see the photo on p. 91). (For information on setting up a power feeder, see Chapter 10.)

Once the frame pieces are shaped, dry-assemble them to check the fit. Then measure for the panel.

Making Panels

When making frame-and-panels, you can make flat panels, which can be plywood and simply inserted into the grooves in the frame. This is a very simple, plain design. But I prefer a more elegant panel: one that is raised. The center, or field, of a raised panel is higher than its edges, creating depth. This is the more traditional design for a frame-and-panel door. Raised panels are easy to create on the shaper, and I'll show you how to do it.

But before we look at shaping the panel, it's important to consider wood movement.

ALLOW FOR WOOD MOVEMENT

Stock for panels should be sized to allow sufficient space for seasonal movement; otherwise, the panel will push the frame apart during the humid summer months. Equally frustrating is having a panel shrink excessively to the point that a gap develops between the panel and a frame member. To be on the safe side, I glue panels to the rails in the middle to force the panel to shrink equally in both directions (see the drawing on the facing page).

When I'm making panels, I usually allow $\frac{1}{16}$ in. on both sides for panel expansion ($\frac{1}{8}$ in. total). I base this upon a 12-in. wide panel and a seven-point swing in moisture content (MC) each year—a low MC of perhaps 5% in dry winter months and a high MC of 12% in summer months. Some wood species, such as curly maple, move more than others and may require an additional $\frac{1}{16}$ in. or so. With the panel cut to size, it's time to raise the field on the shaper.

DEALING WITH WOOD MOVEMENT

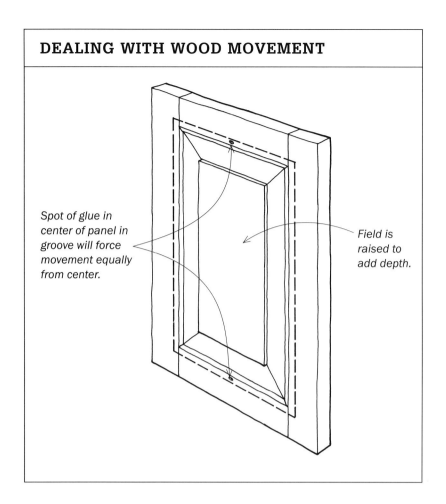

Spot of glue in center of panel in groove will force movement equally from center.

Field is raised to add depth.

RAISING THE FIELD

Panel-raising cutterheads are large in diameter—usually 4½ in. to 5 in.—and so they require a large fence opening. However, a large fence opening exposes the cutterhead to the user's hands and makes it easy for small panels to drop into the cutterhead. I've never felt that inverting the cutterhead to shape panels is a good option, either. Although I've said previously that the cutterhead should always be mounted to cut from underneath the stock, here's an exception. Cutting a panel from underneath can cause variations in the thickness of the panel edge and create a sloppy fit in the frame. Also, when the panel is fed through the shaper facedown, the amount of stock on the table decreases as the bevel is shaped. Small panels are especially difficult to shape facedown as the bearing surface shrinks during shaping.

The box fence completely surrounds the cutterhead and effectively shields your hands at all times during panel-raising.

To allow safe shaping of raised panels faceup, I developed the box fence, which completely surrounds the cutterhead and shields your hands at all times (see the photo above). The panel stock slides under the front of the box fence, so the cutterhead is not exposed. The base of the box is ¼ in. thick and acts as the guide for the stock. And because the base slips underneath the cutterhead, the opening in the base only has to be large enough to accommodate the spindle. Therefore, the opening is small (1 in. for a ¾-in. spindle), and the risk of stock dropping into the cutterhead is drastically reduced. To make this fence, refer to the drawing on p. 17.

Large shapers have the power to raise panels in one pass, but two passes achieves a smoother cut. For the average panel-raising profile, one pass is a heavy cut; the edge of the stock is reduced in thickness by ⅜ in. Removing this much wood in a single cut causes the surface quality to diminish somewhat, even if the shaper has the power to make the cut. I find it's better to take two passes, making the second cut the lighter one. To eliminate tearout on the end grain, shape one of the ends first and then work around the panel.

Shape the lip of the panel to fit snug, but not tight, within the grooves in the frame. A loose panel will rattle within its frame each time the door is opened. On the other hand, forcing the panel into the frame during assembly will most likely cause restriction of movement during seasonal swings in humidity levels. I've found that a friction fit of the panel into the grooves works best.

Making an Arched Frame-and-Panel

For an elegant touch to a raised-panel door, you can arch the panel. The arched frame-and-panel became extremely popular during the 18th century, and it continues to be popular today. It is sometimes referred to as a "tombstone" panel because the design is also found on headstones of the same period.

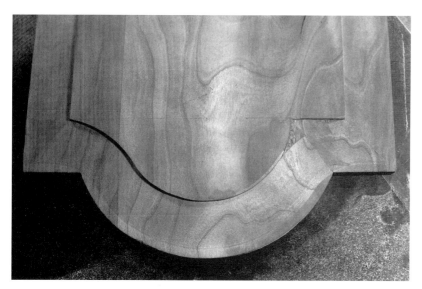

The inside corner on the left of this panel was created on the shaper. To make it an authentic arched raised panel, simply carve the inside corner after shaping (right).

When shaping the top rail (left) and arched panel (right) freehand, use a rub collar and work from the starting pin. A ring guard should also be used.

Original arched panels were segments of a true circle with sharp inside corners where the arc intersected with horizontal shoulders on either side. Today, however, the arch is often reduced to an amorphous curve that lacks the distinction of the originals. This is because classic woodworking designs are often compromised to allow them to be made totally by machine methods. Since the shaper can't create inside corners, the corners on the arched panel are usually eliminated. You can create an authentic arched raised panel, though, if you're willing to combine shaper techniques with a small amount of handwork. You'll simply have to carve the inside corners of the panel after shaping (see the photo on p. 95).

To shape an arched raised panel, follow the procedures outlined earlier in this chapter. The only difference here is that the top rail and the top edge of the panel are arched. If you're using stacked cope-and-stick cutterheads for shaping the frame, then you must use a pattern to shape the top rail. The pattern should have toggle clamps to hold the stock firmly while shaping. If you're using traditional joinery and a stub spindle, you can shape the top rail and the top of the panel freehand. For shaping freehand, you'll need to employ a rub collar and work from a starting pin (see the photos above). For more on shaping curved stock, see Chapter 5. Check the fit of the assembly before carving the inside corners.

9

Sash-Door Joinery

Early woodworkers made large doors with small panes of glass by fitting the glass between molded, interlocking bars. This design was popular for casework such as desks, bookcases and corner cabinets to allow display of contents while keeping out dust. Called a sash door, the design is just as popular today because of the look of distinction it adds to fine furniture and cabinetry. Often, though, the frame pieces consist of just a plywood grid over a large sheet of glass. Making an authentic sash door isn't easy, but it's certainly within the reach of anyone who enjoys crafting fine, detailed work.

A sash-door frame is similar to a frame-and-panel door. However, instead of a wood panel being held in grooves cut into the frame pieces, glass panes are held in rabbets in the frame pieces. In the sash door, molded wood bars separate the glass panes and give the door its distinct appearance. The vertical bars are called mullions, and the horizontal bars are called muntins (see the drawing on p. 98). In an authentic sash door, all frame pieces are joined by mortise-and-tenon joinery with deep mortises and long tenons. I prefer this joinery for sash doors because it has the strength needed to support the heavy weight of the glass. Plus the joints in the frame will be stressed by the weight of the door since the load is supported only on one side from the hinges. This is all the more reason to use mortise-and-tenon joinery in the frame.

A sticking profile is shaped on the inside edges of the stiles and rails and on both edges of the muntins and mullions (for more on

SASH-DOOR ANATOMY

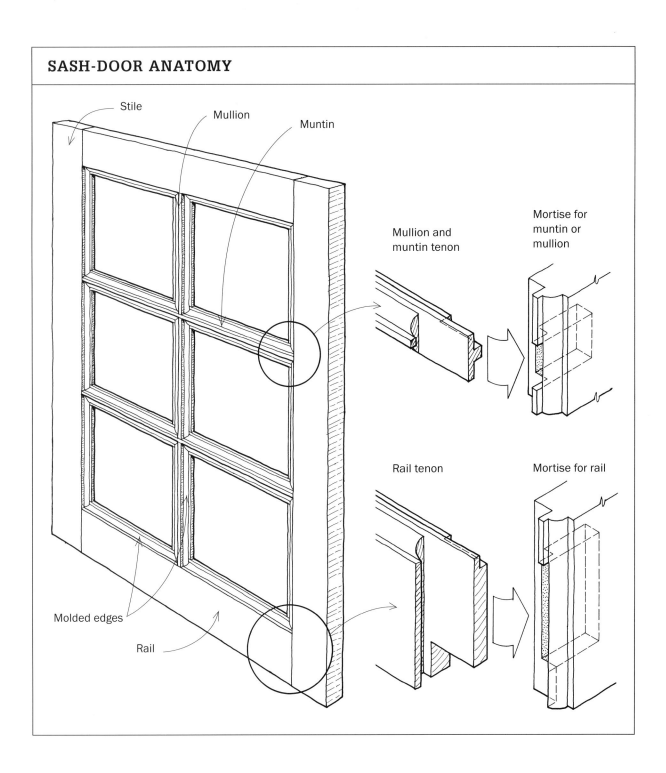

Stile

Mullion

Muntin

Molded edges

Rail

Mullion and
muntin tenon

Mortise for
muntin or
mullion

Rail tenon

Mortise for rail

sticking, see Chapter 8). This molded profile does more than just add decoration; it also reduces the visual mass of the entire frame, giving it a lighter, more delicate appearance without sacrificing strength. I've seen a few old sash doors on provincial cabinets that had square edges instead of a sticking, but this design is unusual (although authentic, the square edges looked harsh and lacked refinement).

Where the sticking intersects in the corners, it must be coped. A coping is simply a reverse profile of the sticking. To create the coping with a long tenon, use a stub spindle and a coping cutterhead on your shaper (for more on shaping with a stub spindle, see pp. 88-89). The first step in creating a sash door is to make a drawing that you can use to select and cut stock to size.

Start with a Drawing

Before cutting stock, make a simple working drawing to clarify the layout and design and provide a reference for the building process. The drawing should show overall dimensions of the door, as well as the dimensions of the stiles, rails, muntins, mullions and sticking profile.

As I mentioned before, the stiles run the entire length of the frame, and rails run horizontally between the stiles. For strength, it's best to divide the mullions into individual segments and mortise them into the muntins. This avoids having long, fragile mullions.

I prefer to make frame members on standard cabinet doors $\frac{7}{8}$ in. thick to better resist warping and for strength. For the average sash door, $\frac{3}{4}$-in. wide mullions and muntins work well with a $\frac{5}{16}$-in. ovolo or thumbnail sticking profile. This creates a small $\frac{1}{8}$-in. fillet in the center of each muntin and mullion, which gives the frame a light look. In my example, both rails and stiles are 2 in. wide.

Selecting and Cutting Stock

With the door dimensions in hand, you're ready to select the stock. To ensure accuracy and a precise fit between frame members, it's important to follow a few precautions. When choosing the stock, be very selective about the wood you use. Carefully examine each piece for straight, clear grain. And if a piece of stock twists or binds during cutting, discard it and select another piece.

Because the muntins and mullions are narrow parts and are difficult to shape, cut them oversize and rip them to finish size later. Rip the stock for these frame members so that you can get two muntins or mullions out of each piece. This will allow you to shape a wider piece of stock. Also, I recommend cutting more stock than you'll need for the mullions and muntins (I usually cut one-and-a-half times what I'll actually need). This will give you a couple of test pieces plus a few extra for insurance. Inevitably, one or two muntins or mullions will break or be slightly misshaped because of their small size. Cutting a few extra muntins and mullions may seem wasteful, but it's much easier than going through the entire procedure a second time.

Making the Frame

Once the stock is properly sized, measure and mark the joint locations on the stock. For accuracy, use a hard (#4) pencil and sharpen it to a chisel edge with fine sandpaper. This may seem extreme, but if all the parts are to fit, it's important to hold to very tight tolerances. You can use a knife to mark the stock if you prefer, but the marks will have to be sanded away.

There are five steps to making a sash-door frame. First lay out the joints. Then cut the mortise-and-tenon joints, shape the coping and sticking profiles and the rabbets, and finally, assemble the frame. Let's look at the frame layout first.

LAY OUT THE JOINTS

Begin the layout with a stile. First mark the door height on the stile (it's also a good idea to double-check to make sure that the finished door will fit the opening). Next, mark the location of the top and bottom rails. Finally, mark each muntin location. Once you've checked your measurements for accuracy, clamp the stiles together and transfer the marks to the opposite stile.

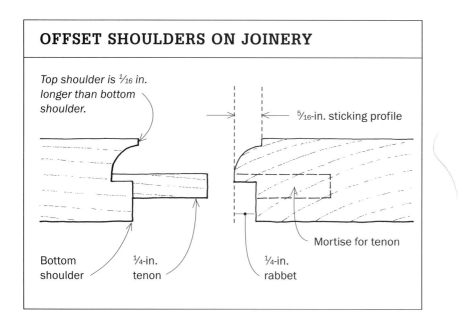

OFFSET SHOULDERS ON JOINERY

Top shoulder is ¹⁄₁₆ in. longer than bottom shoulder.

⁵⁄₁₆-in. sticking profile

Mortise for tenon

Bottom shoulder

¹⁄₄-in. tenon

¹⁄₄-in. rabbet

Lay out the rails next. First find the center of a rail and measure both directions to the tenon shoulders. The top shoulder of each tenon should be ¹⁄₁₆ in. longer than the bottom shoulder because the sticking profile measures ⁵⁄₁₆ in., yet the rabbet measures ¹⁄₄ in. (see the drawing above). If you were to make the sticking profile and rabbet both ¹⁄₄ in., the sticking would be disproportionately small for the size of the muntin and mullion stock. The other option is to make the rabbet ⁵⁄₁₆ in. deep to match the sticking, but this would severely weaken the frame. I think the best choice is to offset the shoulders of the tenon (the size of the offset will depend on the sticking profile).

Finally, mark the mortise locations on the rails and muntins to accept the tenons on the mullions. Again, check your measurements, then clamp the rails together and transfer the marks to the opposite rail. Do the same with the muntins.

The relationship between the mortise, the sticking and the coping is crucial for a clean, well-fitting joint. It's best to position the mortise in the stock flush with the bottom fillet of the sticking profile. To do so, first shape the sticking profiles on the stiles (rails and muntins will be shaped after mortising). Then mark the location of each mortise on each frame piece.

Position the mortise just below the bottom fillet of the sticking profile.

CUT THE MORTISE-AND-TENON JOINTS

After you've laid out all the mortises on the stiles and rails, begin cutting them. When the mortise is properly located, a thin paper edge is all that remains of the fillet on the bottom portion of the sticking (see the photo above). If you'll be shaping two muntins from one piece of stock, remember to mortise all the way through the stock, since it will later be ripped in two.

Cut the long tenons on the table saw for a friction fit with the mortises. Remember to cut the bottom shoulder $\frac{1}{16}$ in. shorter than the top shoulder. To ensure uniformity, use stops on the saw.

CUTTING THE COPING AND STICKING

Because of the length of the tenons in a sash-door frame, it's best to cut the coping with a coping cutterhead mounted on a stub spindle (for more on coping with a stub spindle, see pp. 88-89). A stub spindle is threaded internally, and the cutterhead is secured with a cap screw. Because the cutterhead is counterbored, the head of the cap screw is recessed. This arrangement allows long tenons to pass over the spindle unobstructed. Most shaper manufacturers make a stub spindle as an accessory. (Coping cutterheads are available from shaper tooling catalogs.)

With the shaper off, adjust the height of the spindle so that the top of the cutterhead skims the tenon. Next, position a fence as a depth stop to register against the tenon shoulder so that all cuts are

A piece of ¼-in. plywood clamped to the table serve as the fence and depth stop. It also allows the long tenon to pass over the cutterhead.

identical. A standard fence will not work in this situation because it will not allow the tenon to pass over the spindle. For proper clearance, use a piece of ¼-in. plywood for a fence and secure it to the shaper top with clamps (see the photo above). You'll need to cut a small opening in the plywood for the spindle. Make sure the fence is parallel to the miter-gauge slot so that all copings will be square. Once all the coping is complete, rip the muntin and mullion stock to size on the table saw.

Now shape the sticking profile on the mullions and the muntins (for more on coping and sticking, see Chapter 3). Because the stiles and rails were sticked previously, you can use them to help set up the shaper. Of course, the muntins and mullions are narrow, which makes it difficult to shape them safely and accurately.

A power feeder works well in this situation to hold stock firmly and to guide it past the cutterhead. If you don't own a power feeder, you can use a simple but effective jig for creating the sticking and rabbets on narrow muntins and mullions (see the photo on p. 104). It consists of a rectangular block milled ⅟₃₂ in. thinner than the muntin and mullion stock, with an L-shaped cutout on one edge to accept the stock and a ¼-in. plywood "cap" attached with brads. The cutout should be slightly smaller (about ⅟₆₄ in.) than the width of the stock to be shaped. Because the jig is slightly thinner than the stock, the plywood cap applies downward

This simple jig allows safe shaping of narrow stock and prevents kickback. The stock rides in the L-shaped cutout and is held in place with a ¼-in. plywood "cap."

pressure to hold the stock securely in place. Since no clamps are needed, each piece may be quickly inserted for shaping. An added bonus of the jig is that it prevents kickback (the jig is illustrated on p. 120). To use the jig, place the stock in the cutout, flip the jig, place it against the fence, and you're ready to shape.

CUT THE RABBETS

Once the coping and sticking profiles are shaped, it's time to cut the rabbets to accept the glass. The rabbets for the glass are best cut on the shaper with a square cutterhead. At this point the muntins and mullions are getting smaller and lighter, making them prone to kickback. To avoid a kickback, use the same jig you employed to shape the sticking (see the photo above). In this instance, though, after you've cut the first rabbet, tack a small strip of wood the same thickness as the depth of the rabbet into the jig to fill the rabbet and to provide extra support to the stock (see the photo on the facing page).

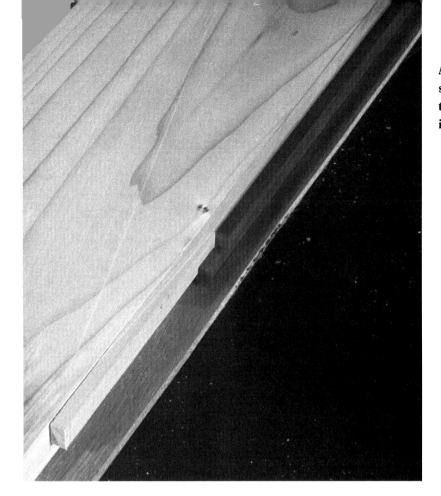

After cutting the first rabbet, tack a small strip of wood the same thickness as the depth of the rabbet into the jig to support the stock.

Before cutting rabbets on all of the stock, shape a test piece first. This is an important step to achieving a good fit at all of the joints. If the rabbet is too deep, the joints will not close on the back of the frame. If the rabbet is too shallow, there will be gaps in all of the joints in the front. Even worse, the frame may not go together at all.

ASSEMBLE THE FRAME

The final step is to assemble the frame. At this point, select the best of the muntin and mullion stock. Assemble the frame pieces without glue to check the fit. Once you're sure that the frame pieces fit snug, glue the door together on a flat surface and allow the glue to dry. If you are skilled at cutting glass, then you can cut the panes $\frac{1}{16}$ in. undersize to fit the frame openings. However, I prefer to let the local glass shop handle this part of the job.

Traditionally, the glass was held in place with putty that was tinted to match the wood. This is also the method that I use, but if you prefer, you can miter small wood strips and tack them in place with small brads to hold the panes. Just be careful not to break the glass or split one of the sash bars.

10

The Power Feeder

The power feeder holds stock firmly against the fence and table and propels it safely past the cutterhead.

The power feeder is one of the most useful accessories you can buy for your shaper (it also can be used on other machines, such as the table saw or jointer). It holds the stock firmly against the fence and table and propels stock safely past the cutterhead (see the photo at left). Like all power tools, a power feeder should be used with caution. But after you gain experience using it, you'll begin to feel at ease and wonder how you ever did without one.

Equipped with a power feeder, your shaper becomes much like an industrial molder capable of efficiently shaping large quantities of stock. I achieve consistent, hands-free results the first time I used a power feeder. Most recently, I used one to shape all the window and door casings for my house. The machine made quick work of what would have otherwise been a long and tiring job.

But a power feeder is not just for production work. Even if you're shaping just a few delicate mullions for a sash door, the power feeder is handy. In this chapter you'll learn about the power feeder's advantages, as well as its anatomy and use. First, let's look at its advantages.

Advantages of a Power Feeder

Most of the shaping I've done through the years has been without a power feeder, so it's certainly not a necessity. However, coupling a power feeder with your shaper certainly has advantages. For instance, it allows you to achieve uniform results consistently while adding an extra safety measure to the shaper. It also allows safe climb-cutting.

UNIFORM RESULTS

Attempting to achieve consistent results on the shaper while feeding stock by hand takes practice, and even with years of experience, I've never been able to achieve the uniform results of a power feeder. Also, a power feeder eliminates the slight burn marks that result from feeding the stock too slow or from pausing to shift hand positions.

Although I always sand molding to smooth away the machine marks from shaping, the time I spend sanding is minimized when I use a power feeder because of the consistency of the surface. A power feeder also eliminates chatter because it holds the stock with much greater force than I can exert with my hands or with any hold-down device, like featherboards or push blocks.

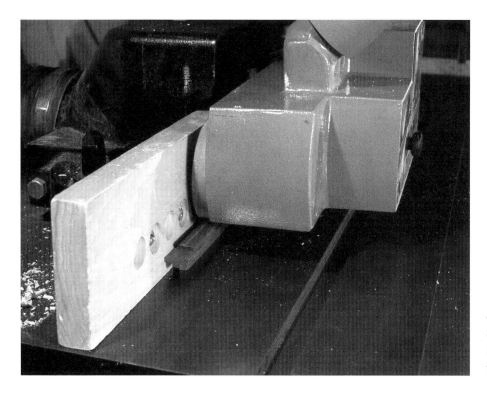

A power feeder holds down narrow stock firmly and maintains pressure throughout the cut.

SAFE SHAPING

Adding a power feeder to your shaper can also give you an extra margin of safety. A power feeder can exert a lot of force, so it's very effective at holding down stock firmly, and it virtually eliminates kickback. Also, when I'm using a power feeder, I no longer need to use other safety devices, such as featherboards and push blocks. Even narrow stock can be shaped safely because the power feeder will grip it firmly and will maintain pressure throughout the cut (see the photo on p. 107). As an added safety benefit, a power feeder shields your hands from the cutterhead and deflects chips toward the dust shroud.

SAFE "CLIMB-CUTTING"

Climb-cutting is the technique of feeding the stock in the same direction as the cutterhead rotation (see the drawing below). Although it is extremely dangerous by hand and should never be attempted (the stock can be quickly pulled into the cutterhead,

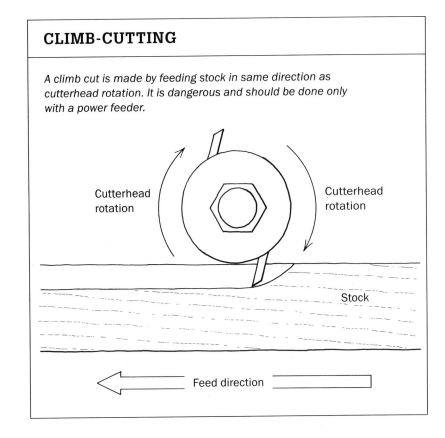

CLIMB-CUTTING

A climb cut is made by feeding stock in same direction as cutterhead rotation. It is dangerous and should be done only with a power feeder.

Cutterhead rotation

Cutterhead rotation

Stock

Feed direction

along with your hands), a power feeder exerts the force necessary to hold the stock firmly.

Climb-cutting leaves a smooth surface free of tearout and chipping because the stock is traveling with the cutterhead rotation, so the wood fibers are sheared cleanly. When climb-cutting, always take light cuts and set the power-feeder speed at the lowest setting.

Power-Feeder Anatomy

Flip through the pages of a catalog, and you'll see that a power feeder is a major purchase, especially if you've just made the plunge into buying a shaper. So before you run out and buy a power feeder, there are a few things you need to know.

The heart of the power feeder is the drive unit. It consists of three or four feed rollers powered by an induction motor (see the photo below), which typically has four or more speeds, usually in the range of 10 to 65 ft. per minute. The drive unit is mounted to horizontal and vertical support columns. The joint between the drive unit and the horizontal column is universal, meaning that it swivels on three different axes. This allows an almost infinite range of adjustment of the drive unit.

Additionally, the unit can be adjusted vertically and horizontally by means of handwheels located at the ends of the support

The drive unit consists of three or four feed rollers powered by an induction motor. It is mounted to horizontal and vertical support columns.

columns. When purchasing a feeder, consider the length of the support columns and the amount of reach that can be obtained with the drive unit. I've found that some low-horsepower (hp) units won't extend far enough forward to shape large stock because the horizontal support column is too short. My advice is to visit a store and see a power feeder mounted on a shaper similar to your own. Make sure that the horizontal support column extends far enough to allow the drive unit to reach past the front of the shaper fence.

Power-feeder motors range in size from ¼ hp to 1 hp. Manufacturers' catalogs will usually suggest a small unit for mounting on a woodworking machine under 5 hp, but this rating is too vague. In general, I've found that a shaper requires a larger, more powerful feeder than a table saw of a similar size. For instance, my 3-hp shaper, when fitted with a large cutterhead, will generate more feed resistance than my 3-hp, 10-in. table saw. If you're doing production work with a 5-hp to 7-hp shaper, you'll definitely want one of the more powerful machines to handle the feed resistance generated by large cutterheads. If you've got a smaller machine like my 3-hp shaper, a power feeder with a ¼-hp motor should suffice.

How to Use a Power Feeder

If you are new to the shaper, then I recommend that you first gain some experience hand-feeding before you try the power feeder. This way you'll get a better feel for feed resistance and gain an understanding of the size cut your shaper is capable of making. I think it's a good idea to take light cuts, even while using a power feeder. This will give you a feel for the power feeder's capabilities as well as for how the shaper and power feeder work together. The setup procedures and speed considerations that follow work for both standard cuts and for climb cuts.

SETUP IS CRITICAL
Mount the base of the power feeder toward the back of the shaper. The location is important: The feeder should clear the fence and dust hood and still reach the front of the fence. I'd suggest that you first secure the base of the feeder with clamps, then, with the shaper turned off, swivel the drive unit into various positions to find the best working location.

Once you've mounted the power feeder, you're ready to set it up and try it out. First, swivel the drive unit into position in front of the cutterhead. Depending on the cut, the wide space between the first two rollers should be located directly in front of the cutterhead so that they can push the stock against the fence or the table.

Angle the drive unit slightly toward the outfeed fence, as shown in the photo above—¼ in. front to rear is usually enough. This will press the stock tightly against the shaper fence and the table.

After angling the drive unit, adjust it for the thickness of the stock to be shaped. Place a test piece between the feed rollers and the table or fence. Then reduce the space by approximately ⅛ in. so that the rollers will compress and grip the stock firmly. Make this adjustment with the handwheels at the end of the support columns. After all the adjustments are made, tighten all the locking levers. Now the power feeder is ready for a test run.

Test the setup with the shaper turned off (and without the cutterhead on the spindle) but with the power feeder on. The stock should stay firmly positioned against the table and fence. If you're shaping long, heavy stock, use a roller stand for support and to prevent the stock from sagging, spoiling the cut. Also, as the feeder is running, try to hold the stock against the force of the motor. If the rollers slip while you're doing this, lower the drive unit a bit to further compress the rollers and to increase their grip. To grip the stock firmly, the feed rollers pivot and compress somewhat. After many hours of use the rollers may become glazed and start to slip. When this happens, use sandpaper to scuff the roller surface for a better grip.

PAY ATTENTION TO SPEED

After making a trial run with the shaper off, it's time to make another trial run with the shaper on. Set the power feeder at the lowest speed and take a light cut. As I mentioned before, a power feeder is equipped with four or more speeds. When you're making multiple passes, use a faster speed for the first cut; then use a slower speed to create a smooth surface on the final pass. Because this is just a test cut, it's okay to use the slow speed initially.

The speed, or feed rate, has considerable impact on the quality of the finished surface. Feeding the stock too fast causes each knife to take a large bite, resulting in a washboard texture. On the other hand, an extremely slow feed rate may cause burning or glazing. Whether I'm hand-feeding or using a power feeder, I aim for 20 to 25 knife marks an inch. This creates a smooth surface that requires very little sanding.

Remember too that the spindle speed and the number of cutters or wings on a cutterhead also affect the surface quality. A fast spindle speed combined with a three- or four-wing cutterhead requires a high feed rate to prevent glazing. Using a two-wing cutterhead, however, will require that you slow down the feed rate to prevent a rough, washboard surface.

11

Shop-Made Jigs for the Shaper

Most woodworkers appreciate a well-made jig. A jig can relieve the tedium of a repetitive task, increase the precision of mating parts and make it possible to machine small or awkward pieces of stock safely. It's true that jigs can expand the possibilities of any woodworking machine; but I think the versatility of the shaper lends itself exceptionally well to the use of jigs. The shaper can accept a wide variety of cutterheads—square cutterheads of various sizes, innumerable profile cutterheads, as well as stacking cutterheads to create several shapes in one pass. To align a jig to the cutterhead, the shaper allows for the use of rub collars, both curved and straight fences, and the miter-gauge slot. This versatility is why I often think of the shaper when a unique machining problem arises.

An assortment of jigs for the shaper are sold through woodworking catalogs or at specialty woodworking stores. These jigs are useful but are limited to specific applications. I do a lot of custom work, and there are times when I need a jig to make the job easier or to provide an extra margin of safety. Because I have a hard time finding manufactured jigs to work on my custom projects, I usually make a jig for any special shaping job that I do.

The V-grooves in this jig align and hold square stock 45° to the square cutterhead for chamfering.

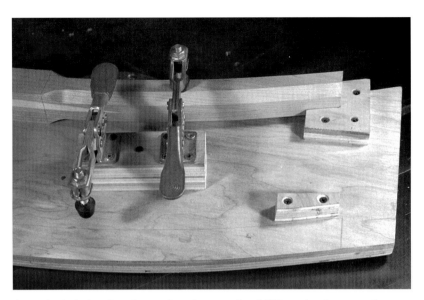

Stop blocks help align the stock to the cutterhead. When shaping curved stock, contour the stop blocks to follow the outline of the workpiece.

Although most woodworkers I meet enjoy the challenge of cobbling up a jig for a specialized job, designing a jig isn't always easy. I can certainly recall times where an idea didn't come to my mind immediately, and I had to walk away from the job for a bit and come back later with a fresh perspective. To give your creative instincts a "leg up," it helps to understand clearly what a jig must do.

Purpose of a Shaper Jig

As I see it, a shaping jig has two important functions. A jig should automatically align the workpiece to the cutterhead and should hold it securely for safe and accurate shaping.

ALIGNING STOCK
For a jig to function effectively, it should align the stock to the cutterhead. That job is best done with the help of stop blocks. All shaping is performed either with a fence or against a rub collar. For shaping straight stock against a fence, stop blocks can be incorporated into the jig to align the stock. When shaping curved stock with a pattern, the stop blocks sometimes must be contoured to follow the outline of the workpiece (see the photo above). (The use of curved stop blocks is illustrated in Chapter 5.)

Sometimes stop blocks must be positioned on the base of the jig to support the stock from underneath. This method is most effective on stock with a compound curve, such as table and chair legs, but it can also be used for stock that must taper in two planes, such as a pencil posts for a bed. Another type of jig uses a series of V-grooves to align stock for shaping (see the photo on p. 113). I find that this jig is ideal for shaping the corners of square stock.

HOLDING STOCK

For a jig to be safe and accurate, it must hold stock against both the lateral and vertical forces of the spinning cutterhead. Lateral forces are simply caused by the cutterhead rotating against the stock. The spinning cutterhead wants to push the stock backward. The vertical forces are caused by vibrations from the spinning cutterhead. Let's look at the lateral forces first.

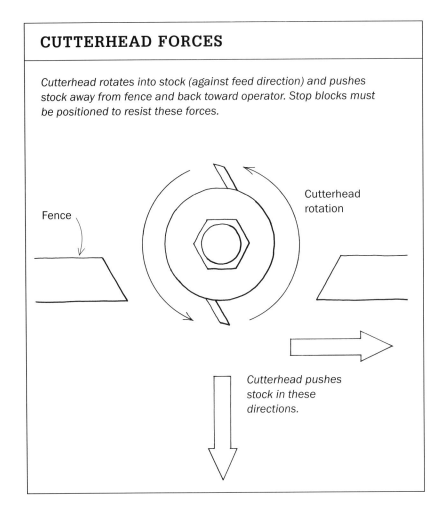

CUTTERHEAD FORCES

Cutterhead rotates into stock (against feed direction) and pushes stock away from fence and back toward operator. Stop blocks must be positioned to resist these forces.

Fence

Cutterhead rotation

Cutterhead pushes stock in these directions.

Toggle clamps exert enough force to hold stock down in a shaper jig, yet they are quick to open and close when changing stock.

Because the spindle is rotating into the stock (against the feed direction), the stock is pushed in two directions—away from the fence and back toward the operator (see the drawing on p. 115). That means the stop blocks not only have to align the stock to the cutterhead, but they also must be positioned on the jig to resist the forces of the spinning cutterhead. To resist those forces, the stop blocks must be placed near the rear of the jig. It's usually not necessary to position stop blocks near the front of the jig to resist the cutterhead forces. However, stop blocks at the front may be necessary to align the stock against the cutterhead, depending on the jig.

Although stop blocks work well to align the stock and hold it against the lateral forces of the cutterhead, they will not prevent the stock from vibrating out of the jig and kicking back. So, in conjunction with the stop blocks, you need some sort of device to hold the stock down in the jig against the vertical forces caused by vibration. The solution I've found that works best is to use toggle clamps.

Toggle clamps are popular for jigs because they exert sufficient force yet are quick to open and close when changing stock. They also are available in various sizes. Because they work so well, I keep several of each size on hand in my shop. A toggle clamp is a very simple device. Its clamping pressure is created by locking a plunger down on the stock (see the photo above). The plunger height can be adjusted by turning a hex screw on the shaft of the plunger. To make adjustments quicker, I replace the hex nut with a wing nut.

When mounting toggle clamps and stop blocks on a shaping jig, make sure they are large enough to resist the lateral and vertical forces of your machine. I know of no specific engineering formulas or rules-of-thumb that can help in this assessment. I just use a good dose of sound judgment (experience will help, too). As always, experiment with light cuts until you get a feel for the setup.

Some Useful Shaper Jigs

For much of the custom work I do, I've had to create special jigs so that the stock could be held safely and securely for the job at hand. Throughout this book I've shown a few of these jigs at work. Most of the jigs were for advanced work, such as shaping multiple curves. However, the three jigs in this section are extremely versatile and can be adapted to a variety of shaping jobs.

A JIG FOR SHAPING TAPERED STOCK

For shaping the octagonal tapers on a pencil-post bed, I frequently use a tapering jig (see the photo below and the drawing on p. 118). The post stock must first be shaped to a four-sided taper, which I

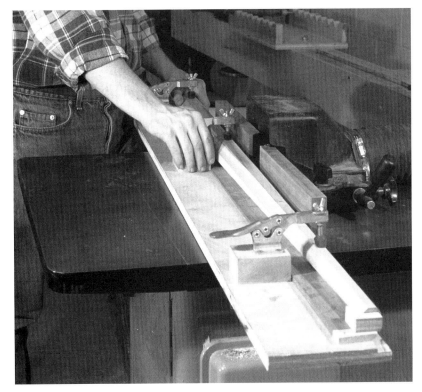

Stop blocks hold the stock in the tapering jig, and three toggle clamps prevent the stock from lifting out of the jig. A long wedge block supports the stock from underneath.

machine on the bandsaw and jointer. Once the initial taper is created, I use the jig with a 45° cutterhead (mounted to cut from underneath) to shape the corners of the post to a tapered chamfer. This jig requires the use of a standard fence (see the photo on the facing page). The fence aligns the stock and jig with the cutterhead.

The unique aspect of this jig is that it supports the tapered stock so that the cutterhead gradually removes more wood as it reaches the end of the cut. A long wedge block fits under the stock at one end to lift the top end of the stock higher off the table (the top end is the thinner end). Stop blocks at the ends and along one edge hold the stock in the jig to resist the vertical forces of the cutterhead. Three equally placed toggle clamps secure the stock against the vertical forces and prevent the stock from lifting out of the jig and kicking back. Although the jig isn't complicated, it substantially reduces the amount of time required to make a pencil-post bed. This jig can also be adapted to shape a wide variety of tapered stock to any profile.

JIG FOR SHAPING TAPERED STOCK

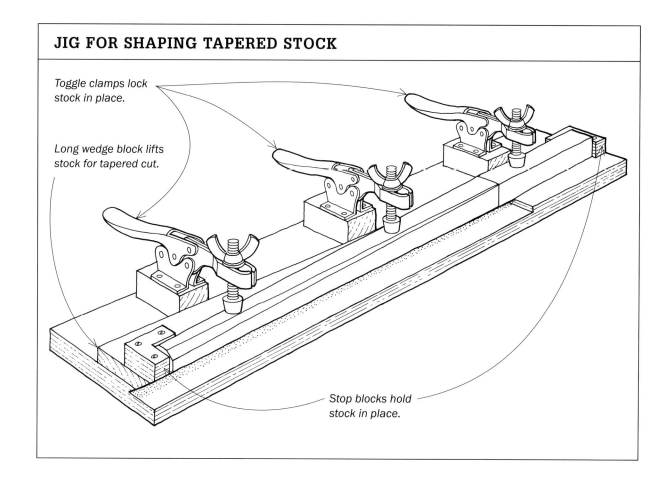

Toggle clamps lock stock in place.

Long wedge block lifts stock for tapered cut.

Stop blocks hold stock in place.

This tapering jig requires the use of a standard fence, which aligns the stock and jig to the cutterhead.

A JIG FOR SHAPING NARROW STOCK

Another of my favorite jigs for shaping narrow stock is the one shown in the drawing on p. 120. I typically use this jig to shape the sticking and rabbets on muntins and mullions for window and door sash (see pp. 104-105), but it can also be used for a variety of shaping jobs on narrow stock. Although simple in design, the jig is very effective at holding stock and keeping it aligned with the cutterhead.

The jig consists of a rectangular block of wood (pine or poplar works fine) that is milled ¹⁄₆₄ in. thinner than the stock to be shaped. On one edge I make an L-shaped cutout the width of the stock, and I cover the rectangular block with a ¹⁄₄-in. plywood "cap." The stock is positioned in the cutout, and the jig is placed against the shaper, with the bottom of the L toward the end of the cut (the lip of the L serves as a stop block). Because the jig is slightly thinner than the stock, the plywood cap will apply downward pressure to hold the stock securely in place. Since no clamps are needed, each piece of stock may be quickly inserted and removed for shaping.

JIG FOR SHAPING NARROW STOCK

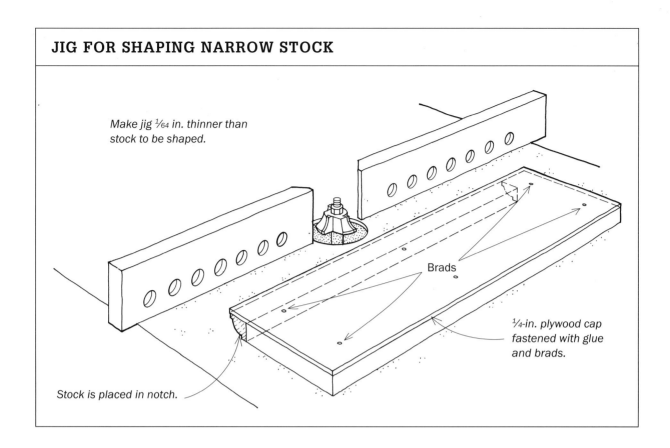

Make jig 1/64 in. thinner than stock to be shaped.

Brads

1/4-in. plywood cap fastened with glue and brads.

Stock is placed in notch.

This jig counteracts the forces of the cutterhead, positions the workpiece and makes a dangerous operation relatively safe. The chatter and kickback inevitable with such a small piece of stock are eliminated.

A JIG FOR SHAPING CORNERS OF SQUARE STOCK

Although a jig with V-grooves is commonly used on a drill press to hold and align stock, it is also an exceptional method to hold and align stock on a shaper (see the drawing on the facing page). I often use this jig to create a stop chamfer on all four corners of a table leg (see the photo on p. 113). The chamfer serves as a decorative element, but it's also necessary for locating cross stretchers under the table. The V-grooves align the legs 45° to the square cutterhead and hold them in that position. This jig could also be used in any situation where a profile is required on the corner of square stock.

JIG FOR SHAPING CORNERS OF SQUARE STOCK

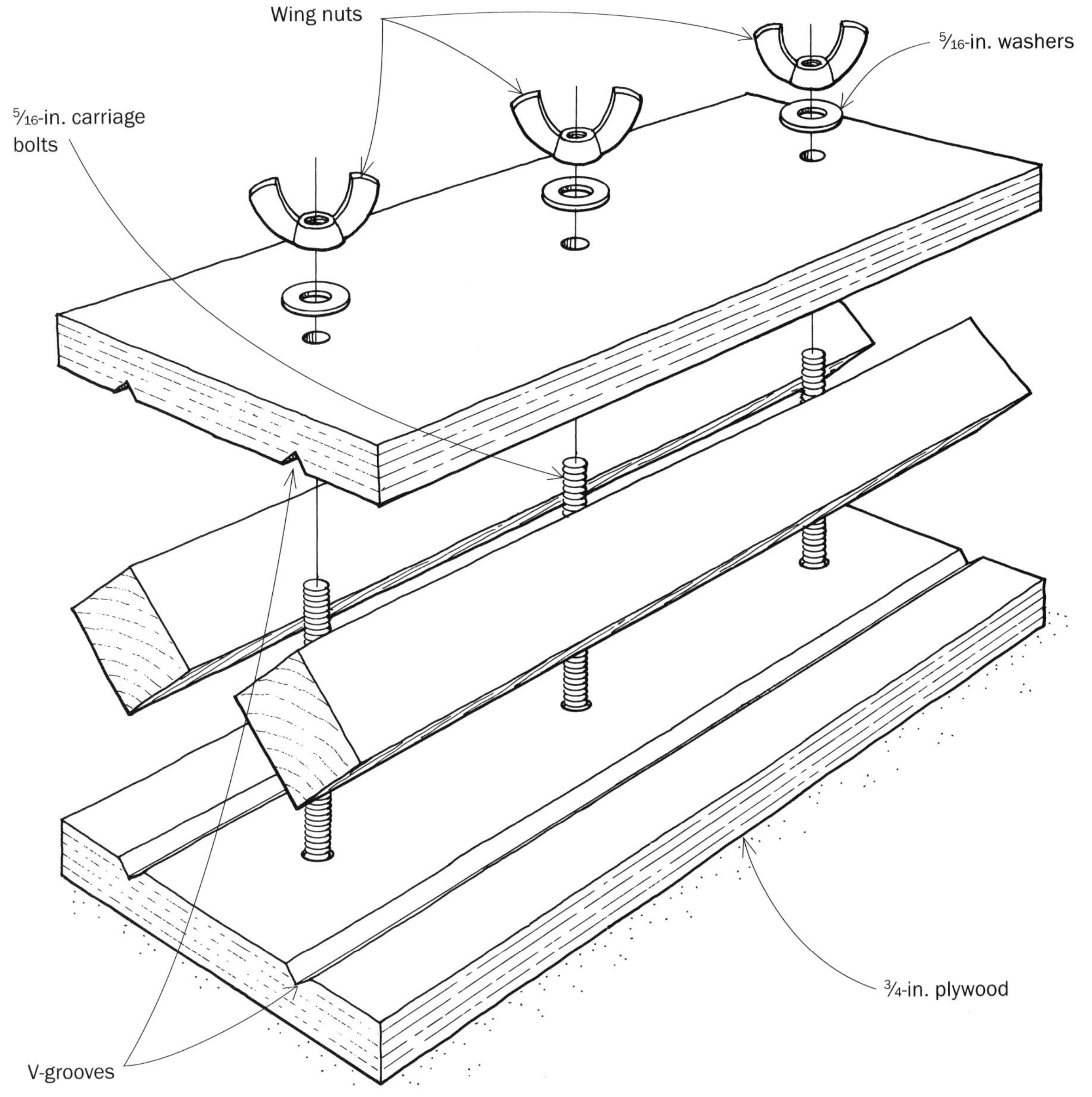

Wing nuts

5/16-in. washers

5/16-in. carriage bolts

3/4-in. plywood

V-grooves

Appendix
Cutterhead Profiles

Amassing a large collection of cutterheads can be expensive. But you can stretch your woodworking dollars by starting with a few basic profiles. These cutterheads can be used separately or combined to create larger, more complicated molding profiles. This appendix shows a few cutterhead profiles that I'd suggest for starting out.

Quarter Round

This cutterhead is extremely versatile because it can be used in three ways. As the name suggests, it can cut a quarter circle, but by adjusting the fence and the spindle, it can also create both thumbnail and ovolo profiles.

The quarter-round cutterhead is available in several sizes, based upon the radius of the quarter circle. It can be used for shaping small applied moldings; it can be combined with other profiles to create complex moldings, such as a sticking profile on door frames; or it can create an edge treatment for tabletops.

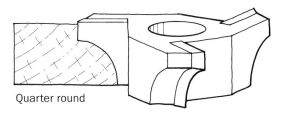
Quarter round

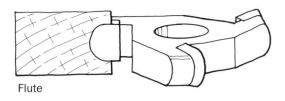

Flute

Flute and Bead

Years ago, woodworkers had sets of wooden molding planes for shaping moldings. Each plane made a different shape as it was pushed across the stock. The most basic of these planes was a complete set of several sizes of hollows and rounds. Today, flute and bead cutterheads are useful in the same way. Both of these profiles can be used independently or combined with other basic profiles to create complex moldings. These cutterheads are sized according to the radius of the profile.

The bead cutterhead can be used for simple or complex moldings, as well as for a sticking profile on panel doors.

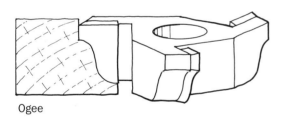

Bead

The fluting profile is most often combined with other shapes to create large moldings. It can also be used for shaping fluted columns and pilasters on both furniture and architecture. Owning several sizes of flute and bead cutterheads will give you the most flexibility.

Ogee

The ogee is another basic profile that can be combined with other cutterheads or used separately for small moldings and edge treatments.

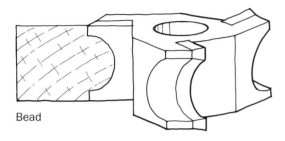

Ogee

Scotia with Bead

This profile is often used as a small molding under a tabletop or chest lid. It's also common to combine it with other profiles to create the molding at the midsection of some case pieces. In architecture, it's used as a backband on window and door casings.

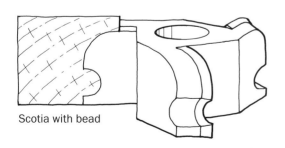

Scotia with bead

Straight

A large (1½ in. to 2 in.) straight cutterhead is useful for pattern shaping and rabbeting. Remember, for pattern shaping, a rub collar must be used.

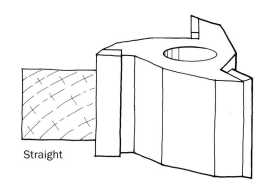

Straight

45° Bevel

This cutterhead can be used to create a variety of chamfers, such as on table edges and pencil-post beds.

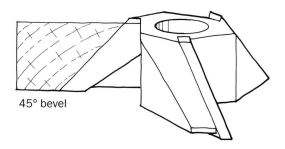

45° bevel

Panel-Raising Cutterhead

Panel-raising cutterheads are available in a wide variety of profiles, but the flat bevel is the most versatile. It may be used with almost any style of furniture or architecture. I prefer cutterheads designated for ⅝-in. thick stock because I typically use a ⅞-in. thick frame.

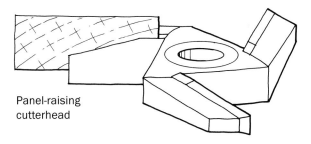

Panel-raising
cutterhead

Glossary

Bead A semicircular or semi-elliptical molding profile, which stands proud of the surrounding surface.

Bead-and-quirk A simple profile consisting of a bead and a shallow groove.

Box fence A shop-made fence designed to surround the cutterhead completely.

Carbide A powder metal with extreme wear resistance, which is brazed on the tips of cutterheads and other wood-cutting devices.

Climb-cutting Feeding stock into the cutterhead in the same direction as the rotation of the spindle. Climb-cutting is dangerous and should only be attempted with a power feeder.

Complex molding A molding profile that is a combination of several basic profiles.

Cope To cut the end of a decorative piece of molding (or frame pieces in frame-and-panel or sash doors and windows) to match the contour of the mating piece (see Sticking).

Cove A simple concave profile consisting of a quarter circle or quarter ellipse.

Cutting angle The angle formed by a radial line drawn from the center of the cutterhead to the face of the knives.

Feed rate The speed in feet per minute (fpm) at which the workpiece is propelled past the cutterhead.

Flute A rounded groove commonly seen on classical architectural columns.

Freehand shaping Shaping curved stock against a rub collar without the aid of a pattern.

Grinding angle The angle formed by the relief bevel and the knife face.

High-speed steel (HSS) A special steel—known for its heat and wear resistance—used for tooling.

Insert cutterhead A cutterhead with knives that lock mechanically into a collar or head.

Insert ring A ring or series of rings that fits into a recess in the shaper table around the spindle so that the shaper can accommodate various sizes of cutterheads.

Keyed lockwasher A special washer with a nib that engages with a groove in the spindle to prevent the spindle nut from backing off.

Lockedge collar Part of an insert cutterhead that secures the knives with a worm screw that engages with serrations in the knives.

Lockedge knives Insert tooling designed for use with lockedge collars. These knives are typically made of high-speed steel, which can be ground to a profile by the user.

Matching cutterheads A set of cutterheads, with each cutterhead designed to cut the opposite profile of the other, i.e., tongue-and-groove, cope-and-stick.

Mullion A vertical inside frame member that separates wooden panels or panes of glass.

Muntin A horizontal inside frame member that separates wooden panels or panes of glass.

Ogee A flowing S-curved profile—convex on top and concave on the bottom.

Ovolo A simple profile that consists of a semicircle and two fillets.

Pattern A template for freehand shaping that secures the workpiece and guides it past the cutterhead safely. The base of the pattern follows a rub collar.

Pattern shaping Shaping curved stock freehand with the aid of a pattern.

Power feeder An accessory that mounts to the shaper table and mechanically propels the stock past the cutterhead.

Quarter round A simple molding profile of a quarter circle.

rpm Refers to the speed of the spindle or motor in rotations per minute.

Rabbet A square or rectangular recess along the edge or end of a board.

Rail A horizontal member of a frame in frame-and-panel or stile-and-rail construction.

Relief bevel A shallow angle on cutting surfaces of a knife perpendicular to the spindle, which prevents the knife from rubbing the stock during each revolution.

Reverse ogee A flowing S-curved profile—concave on top and convex on the bottom.

Rim speed The speed of a cutterhead at the periphery.

Ring guard A soft metal or hard plastic ring suspended over the cutterhead as a guard when shaping curved stock.

Rub collar A collar with ball bearings placed above or below the cutterhead to limit the cut when shaping curved work.

Scotia A simple concave molding profile.

Spindle The threaded steel shaft on which the cutterhead is mounted.

Split fence A fence with infeed and outfeed halves that are independently adjustable.

Stacking cutterhead Two or more separate cutterheads designed to be stacked together on the spindle to shape one complex profile.

Starting pin A short, tapered or threaded steel rod that mounts near the cutterhead for supporting curved stock when shaping freehand.

Steel collar A steel ring used as a spacer for positioning the cutterhead at the correct height on the spindle.

Sticking The molded profile on the inside edges of a frame that matches the coped profile on the ends of mating frame pieces. Used in both sash doors and frame-and-panel construction, the sticking must be mitered or coped in the corners.

Stile A vertical member of a frame in stile-and-rail construction.

Stop cut A cut that starts and/or stops before reaching the ends of the workpiece.

Stub spindle A short spindle designed for use with a cope cutterhead for coping the ends of rails and muntins. It allows long tenons to pass over the cutterhead.

Thumbnail A simple profile that consists of a semicircle or semiellipse and a fillet.

Wing cutterhead A one-piece cutterhead with two or more cutting surfaces.

Sources

Shapers

**Delta International
Machinery Corp.**
246 Alpha Drive
Pittsburgh, PA 15238
(800) 438-2486

Grizzly Imports, Inc.
P.O. Box 2069
Bellingham, WA 98227
(800) 541-5537

Powermatic
619 Morrison Street
McMinnville, TN 37110
(615) 473-5551

Cutterheads

Amana Tool Corp.
120 Carolyn Boulevard
Farmingdale, NY 11735
(800) 445-0077

CMT Tools
310 Mears Boulevard
Oldsmar, FL 34677
(800) 531-5559

**Freeborn Tool
Company, Inc.**
N. 6202 Freya Street
P.O. Box 6246
Spokane, WA 99207
(800) 523-8988

Freud USA, Inc.
218 Feld Avenue
High Point, NC 27264
(800) 472-7307

MLCS, Ltd.
2381 Philmont Avenue
Huntingdon Valley, PA 19006
(800) 533-9298

Charles G.G. Schmidt & Co., Inc.
301 West Grand Avenue
Montvale, NJ 07645
(800) 724-6438

Index

Publisher: JAMES P. CHIAVELLI

Acquisitions Editor: RICK PETERS

Publishing Coordinator: JOANNE RENNA

Editor: THOMAS C. McKENNA

Layout Artist: ROSALIE VACCARO

Photographer, except where noted: LONNIE BIRD

Illustrator: VINCE BABAK

Typeface: PLANTIN

Paper: 70-LB. MOISTRITE MATTE

Printer: QUEBECOR PRINTING/HAWKINS, NEW CANTON, TENNESSEE